HAL LEONARD
GUITAR METHOD

Supplement to Any Guitar Method

BLUEGRASS GUITAR

BY FRED SOKOLOW

Speed • Pitch • Balance • Loop

To access audio visit:
www.halleonard.com/mylibrary

Enter Code
2898-2511-9975-8375

with editorial assistance by Ronny Schiff

ISBN 978-1-4234-9161-3

7777 W. BLUEMOUND RD. P.O. BOX 13819 MILWAUKEE, WI 53213

Visit Hal Leonard Online at
www.halleonard.com

CONTENTS

INTRODUCTION

Welcome to the *Hal Leonard Bluegrass Guitar Method*. This book covers bluegrass backup and lead. It can be useful for players at all levels, as it starts with basic accompaniment and works its way up to advanced soloing concepts. If you're a beginner, start with the "Accompaniment" section. Intermediate or advanced players need not follow the book in chronological order, but they'll find plenty of helpful ideas on improvisation and lead playing in the "Soloing" section.

ABOUT THE AUDIO 🔊

The accompanying tracks contain audio for nearly all the written music examples in this book. The corresponding track number for each song or example is listed below the audio icon. All guitar parts are panned to one side of the stereo mix, so you can isolate them for close study or pan them out to play along with the band.

Guitar, banjo, mandolin: Fred Sokolow
Sound engineer and bass: Michael Monagan
Recorded and mixed at Sossity Sound, Culver City
Mastered by WMG Mastering

THE ROLE OF THE GUITAR IN BLUEGRASS

Although bluegrass clearly has its roots in centuries-old mountain music, most bluegrassers would agree that the genre crystallized around 1946 when Bill Monroe, already a legendary Opry star, began performing and recording with his new band lineup that included Earl Scruggs on 5-string banjo and Lester Flatt on guitar. By the end of the decade, countless acoustic string bands were springing up all over the South imitating Monroe's musical format and style. The public began referring to them as "bluegrass" bands, as they were clearly of the same ilk as Bill Monroe and the Bluegrass Boys (so named because Monroe hailed from the state of Kentucky).

Bluegrass was noted for rapid tempos, tight vocal harmonies, and hot instrumental solos. Monroe had his soloing instruments (fiddle, mandolin, and banjo) take turns, so that each had its moment in the spotlight. This naturally encouraged virtuoso picking, but for many years, the guitar served as a rhythm instrument and almost never played a solo—unless you count Lester Flatt's famous *G run*, the brief musical phrase that signaled the end of a chorus or solo. The G run became an essential part of bluegrass music.

In the early 1960s, Doc Watson and Clarence White stunned the bluegrass audience and guitar pickers everywhere by flatpicking dazzling fiddle tunes as well as trading hot instrumentals during vocal numbers with the fiddle, banjo, and other soloists. Just as Earl Scruggs spawned a new generation of three-finger banjo pickers, Doc Watson and Clarence White gave birth to a new type of bluegrass guitarist who played rhythm but also tore off hot solos just like the other virtuoso pickers in the band.

In order to play guitar in today's bluegrass band, you're expected to hold down the rhythm (and make it cook!) and to play a hot solo now and then—no faster than a runaway locomotive. Often, the guitarist is the main singer in the band as well.

RECOMMENDED LISTENING

Everybody learns by imitating, and the best way to start learning bluegrass guitar is to listen to the greats of the present and past, including the pre-bluegrass guitarists who influenced them. Here are some of the most important names:

Maybelle Carter's playing with the original Carter Family in the 1930s defined country guitar for many years. She was probably the first acoustic country guitarist to record a solo, and her backup style (the *Carter strum*) and solos were widely imitated. So was the backup playing of **Riley Puckett** (with Gid Tanner and the Skillet Lickers), whose long bass runs and rhythm style inspired many a guitar picker in the thirties, forties, and beyond. **Charlie Monroe**'s rhythmic strumming with the Monroe Brothers (in the thirties) also helped set the stage for bluegrass guitar.

The 1950s are widely regarded as the golden age of bluegrass. **George Shuffler** played guitar solos with the Stanley Brothers, but he was the exception that proved the rule; **Carter Stanley** and nearly every other bluegrass guitarist of this era played rhythm, including **Lester Flatt** (of Flatt and Scruggs and the Foggy Mountain Boys), **Jimmy Martin**, **Red Smiley** (of Reno and Smiley), and a long list of guitarists who played with Bill Monroe and the Bluegrass Boys. During his career, Flatt played solos on only two songs, and they were identical (the same solo fit neatly in both tunes)! Nevertheless, in the fifties' recordings, you can hear the guitar subliminally driving these bands, creating the rhythm and punctuating the sections of songs with G runs—the rhythm guitar was the locomotive that pulled the train.

Doc Watson's Vanguard recordings and **Clarence White**'s picking with the Kentucky Colonels launched the bluegrass guitar as a soloing instrument. Pickers of note who followed include **Dan Crary**, **Norman Blake**, **Tony Rice** and, later, **Bryan Sutton**, **David Grier**, **Dan Tyminski**, **Steve Kaufman**, and a lot more.

WHAT TYPE OF GUITAR TO USE

Traditionally, bluegrass guitarists have played dreadnought Martin steel-string guitars, partly because they are excellent, loud guitars with a stronger bass and midrange than most steel-stringed acoustics, and because everybody else played one! This type of instrument is still far and away the first choice of most bluegrassers, but many companies besides Martin are making them, including Collings, Laravee, Santa Cruz, and Bourgeois.

FLATPICKS AND FINGERPICKS

Martin D-28

Carter Stanley, Lester Flatt, and many other bluegrass guitar pioneers played with a thumbpick (usually plastic) and one or two metal fingerpicks. Today, most players use a flatpick—especially guitarists who play fast solos and fiddle tunes. Bluegrass players favor a heavy flatpick that doesn't bend. Here are some of the more popular pick shapes and how they're held (or worn):

Finger Picks and Thumb Pick

Various Flatpicks

Wearing Picks

Holding Pick

Thumbpicks come in different sizes. Metal fingerpicks can be bent to fit different size fingers.

ACCOMPANIMENT

Learning basic accompaniment is a good way to begin learning bluegrass guitar, even if your goal is to be a hot soloist. While learning backup, you'll acquire the chords, bass runs, and rhythmic strums needed for lead playing as well. Besides, in a jam session or performance with other pickers, players tend to swap solos in a given song. As a result, the guitarist and all the other instruments spend more time playing backup than soloing. And the best way to begin playing backup is to learn the *Carter strum*.

BASIC CARTER STRUM

The basic bluegrass guitar strum closely resembles the Carter strum Maybelle played. It goes like this:

1. Pick the bass note (for example, the 6th string of a G chord).
2. Pick down–up on the top three or four strings.

TRACK 1

If you use a flatpick, those three strokes are performed with the pick going down–down–up. If you use a thumbpick and fingerpicks, play the downstrokes with your thumb and the upstroke with your index finger.

ALTERNATING BASS

The Carter strum isn't complete until you start alternating bass notes. Follow steps 1–2, then:

3. Pick another bass note, preferably the 5th of the chord (for example, the open 4th string of a G chord).
4. Pick down–up on the top three or four strings.

TRACK 1
(0:09)

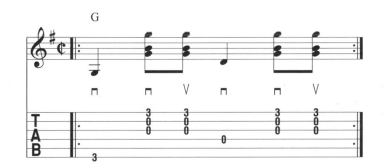

Here's backup for "Blue Ridge Cabin Home," a tune Flatt and Scruggs made famous. The simple backup part consists of the Carter strum with alternating bass. The first version, in the key of G, uses these three chord shapes:

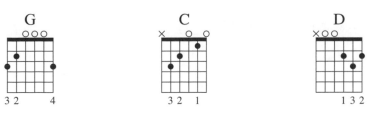

If these chords are new to you, practice switching from one to the other while strumming a steady rhythm, like this:

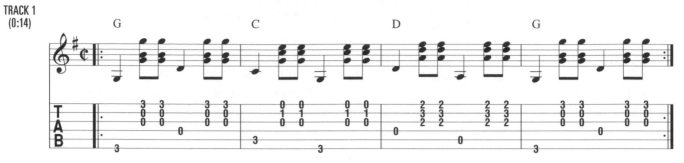

Now play "Blue Ridge Cabin Home" in G and notice which alternating bass notes are played for each chord.

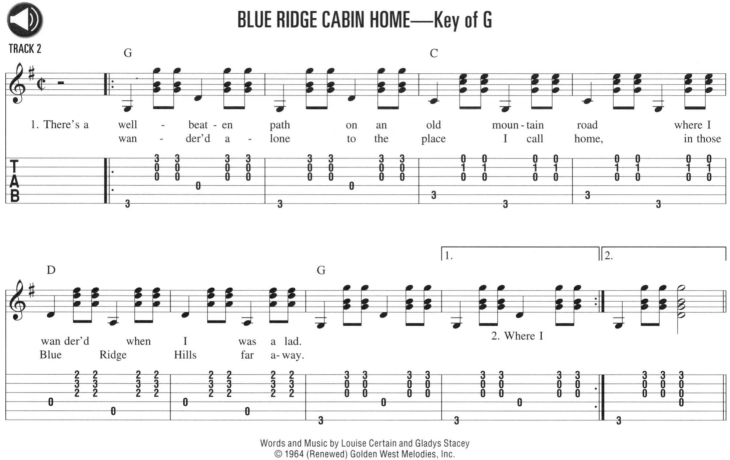

BLUE RIDGE CABIN HOME—Key of G

TRACK 2

1. There's a well - beat - en path on an old moun - tain road where I
   wan - der'd a - lone to the old place I call home, in those

wan der'd when I was a lad.
Blue Ridge Hills far a- way.

2. Where I

To play the same tune in C, you'll need one new chord: F. Some people barre the 1st fret with their index finger, while others catch the 6th string with their thumb (reaching over the neck of the guitar). If you use the "thumb" method, mute the 5th string by touching it with your ring finger:

BLUE RIDGE CABIN HOME—Key of C

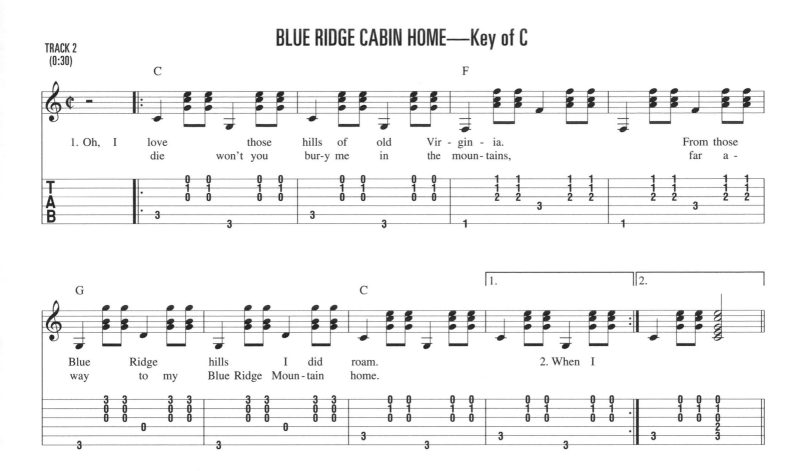

1. Oh, I love those hills of old Vir-gin-ia. From those
   die won't you bur-y me in the moun-tains,

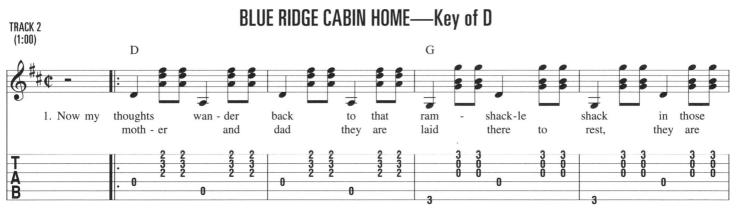

Blue Ridge hills I did roam. 2. When I
way to my Blue Ridge Moun-tain home.

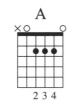

A

To play the song in the key of D, you need an A chord:

2 3 4

BLUE RIDGE CABIN HOME—Key of D

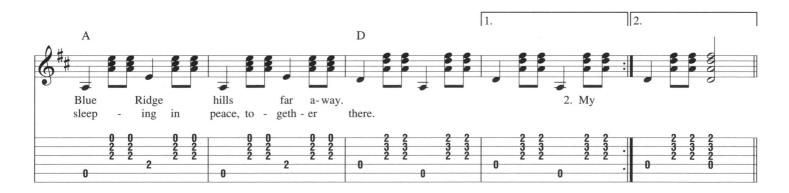

1. Now my thoughts wan-der back to that ram - shack-le shack in those
   moth - er and dad they are laid there to rest, they are

Blue Ridge hills far a-way. 2. My
sleep - ing in peace, to - geth - er there.

SLOWER TEMPO/BASIC STRUM

When playing songs with a slower tempo, most pickers fill up the empty space with more upstrokes. The basic pattern changes slightly:

1. Pick the root (bass) note.
2. Pick up–down–up on the top three or four strings (sometimes the first upstroke is omitted).
3. Pick another bass note, preferably the 5th of the chord (for example, the open 4th string in a G chord).
4. Pick up–down–up on the top three or four strings.

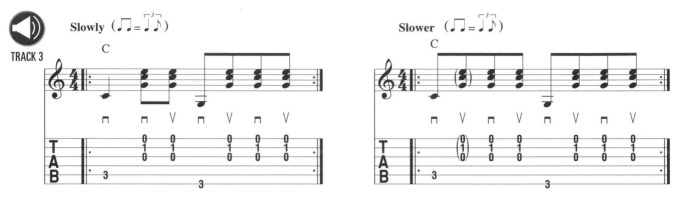

As with the basic strum, flatpickers perform all the above strokes with a pick. If you use a thumbpick and fingerpicks, play the downstrokes with your thumb and the upstrokes with your index finger.

The first upstroke in the slower pattern is written in parentheses because it's often omitted. It's only needed for very slow tempos.

The next song, "Long Black Veil," was made popular by the great honky-tonk country singer, Lefty Frizell. It has become a standard in the bluegrass repertoire, and several rock bands (the Band, the Grateful Dead, and others) have recorded it as well. It's usually played at a moderate tempo and calls for the "enhanced basic strum" that includes the extra upstroke. This version is in the key of E, so you'll need two new chord shapes. Practice switching from one to the other several times if they're unfamiliar to you:

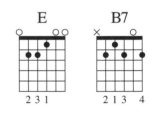

THE LONG BLACK VEIL—Key of E

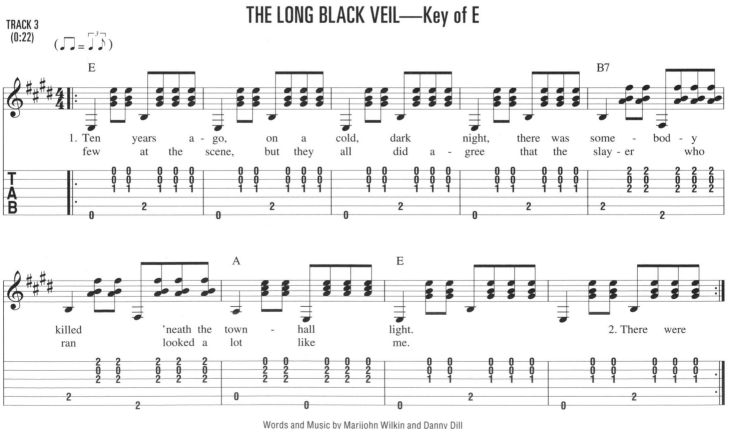

The following version of the Flatt and Scruggs tune, "We'll Meet Again Sweetheart," is played at a slow enough tempo to require the basic strum with two upstrokes added. It's in the key of A:

WE'LL MEET AGAIN SWEETHEART—Key of A

TRACK 4

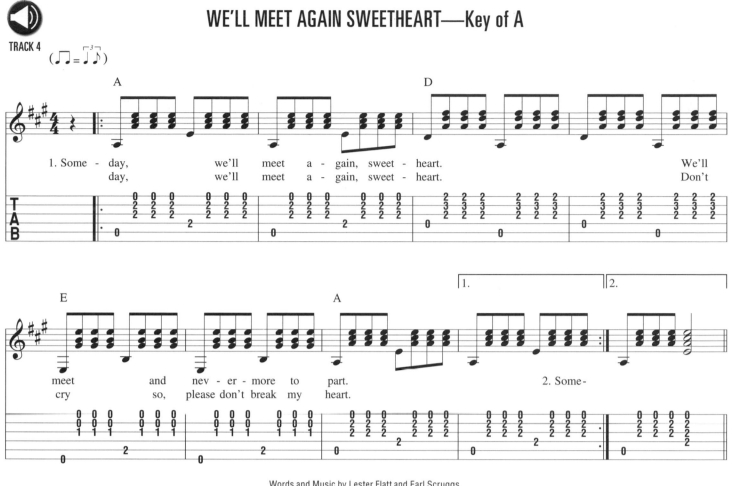

meet / cry ... and / so, ... nev-er-more / please don't break to / my ... part. / heart. ... 2. Some-

THE G RUN

The *G run*, popularized by Lester Flatt, is played at the end of a verse or chorus. There are many variations of the lick; here are a few:

TRACK 5

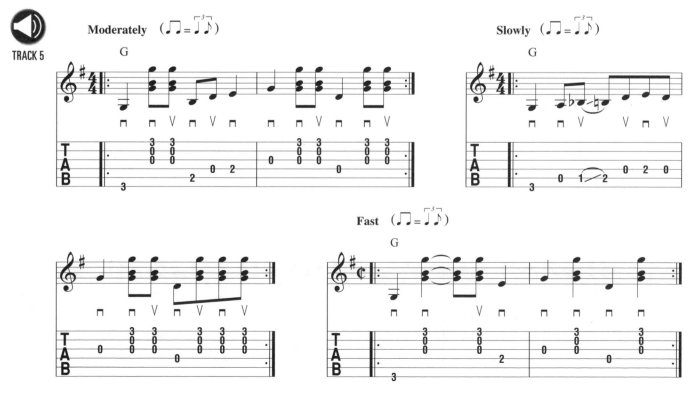

Here's how the G run sounds in "We'll Meet Again Sweetheart," played at three different speeds. In each case, it comes at the end of the chorus:

TAG ENDINGS IN OTHER KEYS

The G run is basically a "tag ending" that wraps up a verse or chorus. It can be adapted to other keys as well:

D Tag Endings

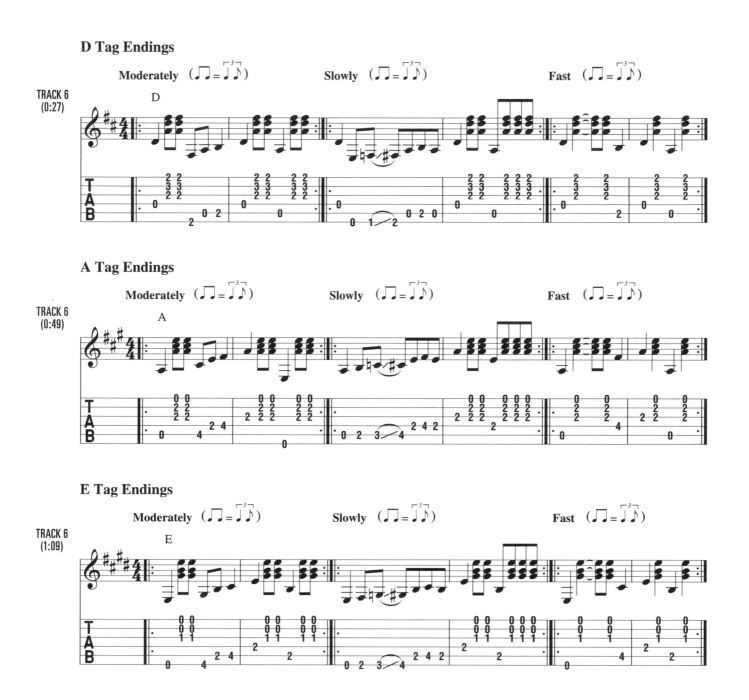

A Tag Endings

E Tag Endings

BASS RUNS

Bluegrass rhythm guitarists often play *bass runs* to connect one chord to another. A bass run is a series of notes, played on the lower strings, that is usually part of a major scale. For example, here are two typical bass runs that connect a G chord to a C chord. The first is a portion of a G major scale. The second is a variation that includes an extra note:

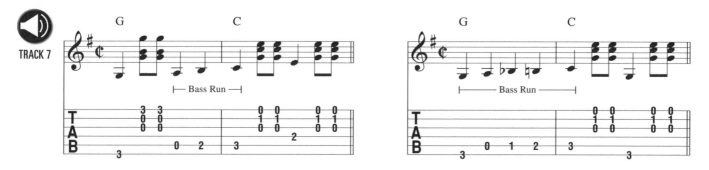

Bass runs are especially appropriate during a pause in a vocal line, but they can be played anytime you go from one chord to another. Here's the backup to a very popular gospel tune, "I'll Fly Away," in several keys, with all the bass runs it can hold (more than you'd normally want to play!):

I'LL FLY AWAY—Key of D

I'LL FLY AWAY—Key of E

I'll   fly   a   -   way   oh,   glor - y.

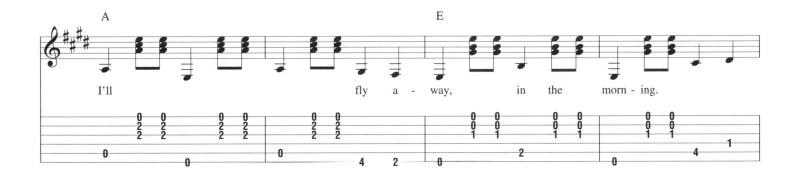

I'll   fly   a   -   way,   in   the   morn - ing.

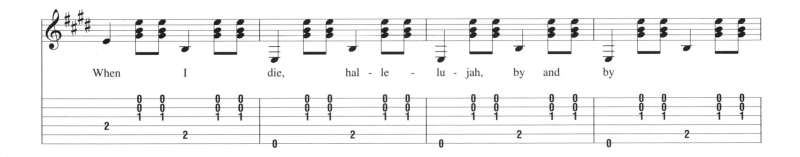

When   I   die,   hal - le - lu - jah,   by   and   by

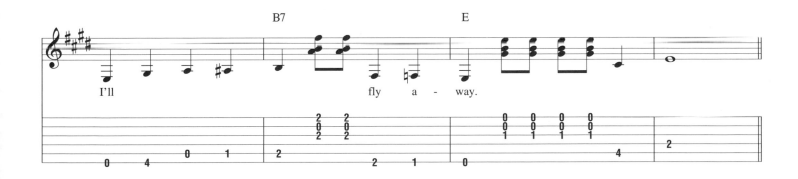

I'll   fly   a - way.

I'LL FLY AWAY—Key of C

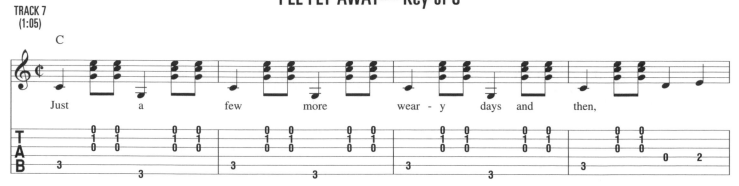

Just a few more wear - y days and then,

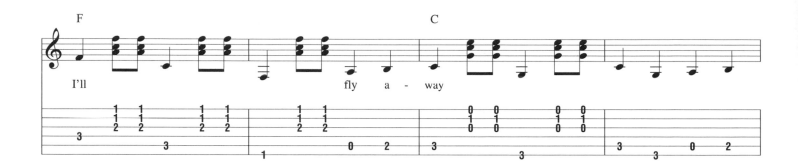

I'll fly a - way

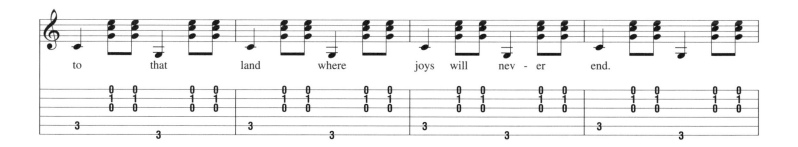

to that land where joys will nev - er end.

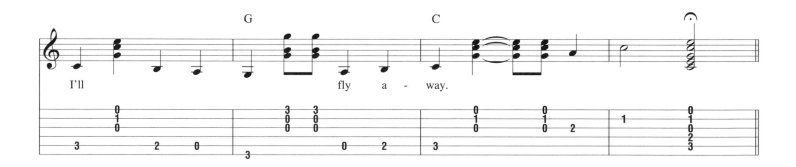

I'll fly a - way.

"Salty Dog," another bluegrass standard, has room for plenty of bass runs:

SALTY DOG BLUES—Key of G

TRACK 8

1. I'm stand-in' on the corner with the low - down blues, great big hole in the bot - tom of my shoes.
2. Let me be your sal-ty dog, or I won't be your man at all.

Hon - ey let me be your sal - ty dog.

WALTZ BASIC STRUM

Here's the basic bluegrass strum, adapted to *waltz* (3/4) time:

1. Pick the root bass note.
2. Pick (up)–down–up–down–up on the top three or four strings.
3. Pick another bass note, preferably the 5th of the chord (for example, the open 4th string in a G chord).
4. Pick (up)–down–up–down–up on the top three or four strings.

Those upstrokes in parentheses are only needed for very slow tempos. You can also play brisk (faster) waltz tempos with no upstrokes:

1. Pick the root bass note.
2. Pick down–down on the top three or four strings.
3. Pick another bass note, preferably the 5th of the chord (for example, the open 4th string in a G chord).
4. Pick down–down on the top three or four strings.

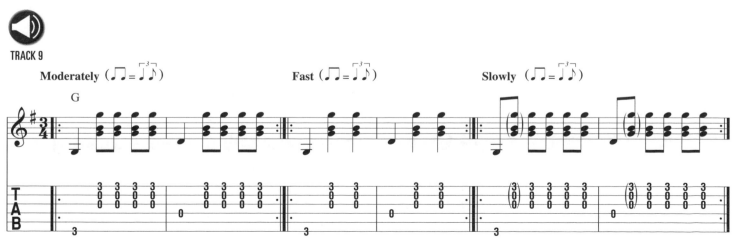

TRACK 9

Moderately   Fast   Slowly

TAG ENDINGS IN WALTZ TIME

Tag endings can be adapted to waltz time with a few slight changes:

Here's a Bill Monroe signature waltz tune, "Blue Moon of Kentucky," played in two keys:

BLUE MOON OF KENTUCKY—Key of G

TRACK 10

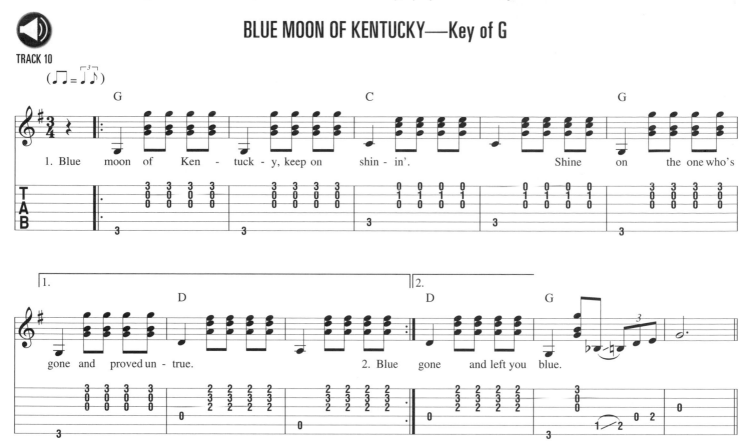

BLUE MOON OF KENTUCKY—Key of D

TRACK 10
(0:30)

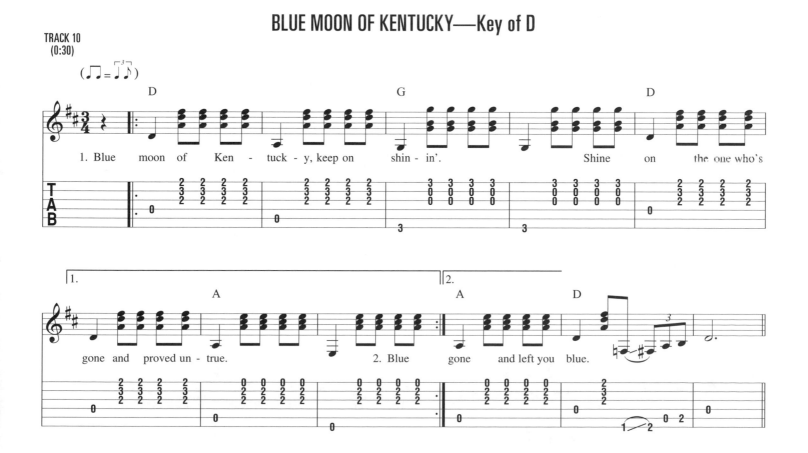

BASS RUNS IN WALTZ TIME

Bass runs also change slightly to adapt to 3/4 time. Here's the guitar backup for the well-known gospel tune, "Amazing Grace," in several keys with bass runs and tag endings:

AMAZING GRACE—Key of C

TRACK 11

AMAZING GRACE—Key of D

TRACK 11
(0:31)

AMAZING GRACE—Key of E

CHORD FAMILIES AND THE I–IV–V CONCEPT

The chords in songs are not random. Nearly every song has a repeated chord pattern. For instance, in the key of G, "Blue Ridge Cabin Home" has the chord sequence G–C–D–G over and over, and each chord is two measures long.

You may have also noticed that most of the songs in this book have three chords. That's because chords tend to form three-chord "chord families." In every key, there are three chords that are most likely to occur, and they can be regarded as an immediate family. For instance, all the songs you've played so far that are in the key of G have a G, a C, and a D chord. G, C, and D are the immediate G "chord family." Countless songs in the key of G contain these three chords.

Bluegrass players, and musicians in general, often think of chord progressions in terms of numbers. Instead of describing a song with letter names (G, C, and D), they talk about "one, four, and five chords." That's because in any key, the immediate chord family consists of one, four, and five. The numbers refer to the major scale of a song's key. The first note in the G major scale is G, so in the key of G, a G chord is called the "I chord" (Roman numerals are used in this context). The fourth note in the G major scale is C, so C is the "IV chord," and so on. In the key of E, E is the first note in the E major scale, A is the fourth note, and B the fifth, so E, A, and B are *I*, *IV*, and *V* in the key of E.

All chord progressions can be expressed with numbers. It's a helpful way to talk or think about songs, because the IV chord has a certain *sound* in relation to the I chord, and so does the V chord. When you start thinking in terms of numbers (*intervals*, or spaces between notes), you're understanding fully how a song *works*. Also, when you express a tune this way ("Now go to the IV chord…") it fits any key.

Here's a chart of chord families in the easiest guitar keys:

I	IV	V
C	F	G
G	C	D
D	G	A
A	D	E
E	A	B7

21

Note: B7 is usually played instead of B because it's an easier chord to play. B is a barre chord, and B7 doesn't require a barre.

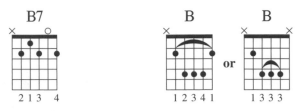

TYPICAL PROGRESSIONS

I–IV–V–I: Many songs follow the "Blue Ridge Cabin Home" formula, although the measure count isn't always the same. For example, the well-known "I Am a Man of Constant Sorrow" has this pattern: four measures of I, two measures of IV, two measures of V, two measures of I. That final "two measures of I" isn't fixed in stone, because it's a common convention in bluegrass to hang on that final I chord for as long as it takes the singer to begin another verse.

Here's a backup guitar part for "I Am a Man of Constant Sorrow" in three keys, so that you can get some more practice with bass runs and tag endings. The song, recently popularized in the film *O Brother, Where Art Thou?* is at least a hundred years old. It was popularized in the early 1950s by the Stanley Brothers and has been recorded by numerous artists over the years; there's a frenetic version on Bob Dylan's 1962 debut album. The arrangement that follows is the Soggy Mountain Boys version.

Because "I Am a Man of Constant Sorrow" has a strong blues inflection, it includes some seventh chords:

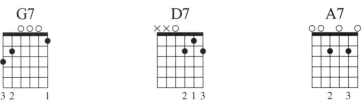

I AM A MAN OF CONSTANT SORROW—Key of G

TRACK 12

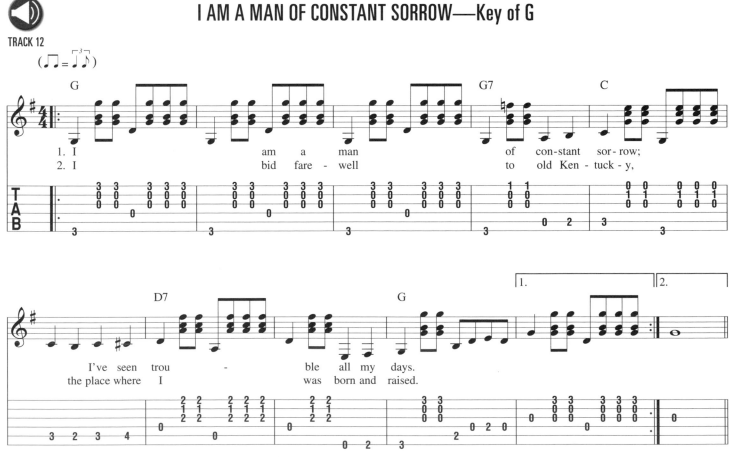

I AM A MAN OF CONSTANT SORROW—Key of D

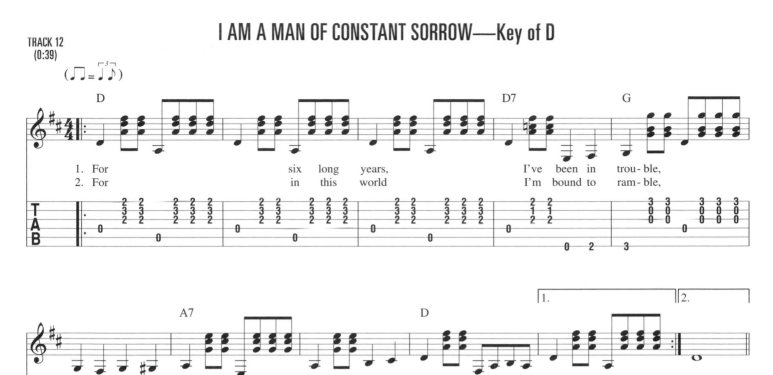

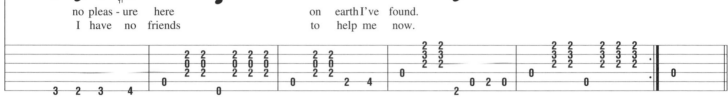

I AM A MAN OF CONSTANT SORROW—Key of A

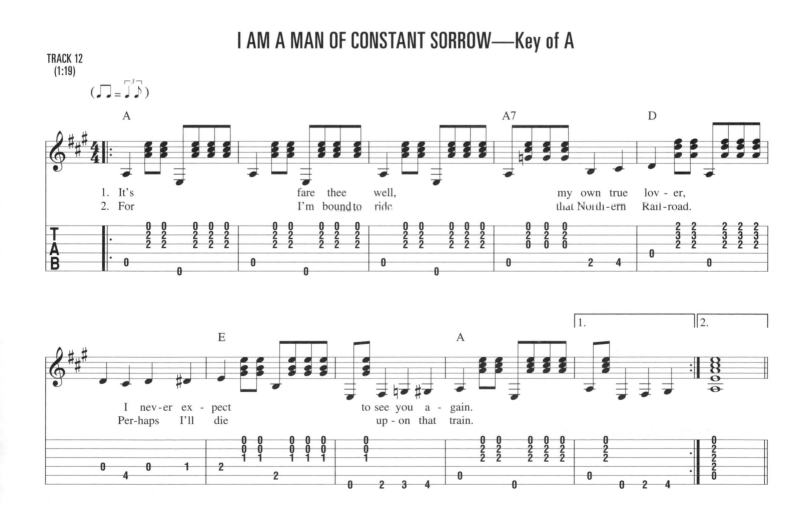

Other popular bluegrass tunes with this chord progression include "Wabash Cannonball," "You Don't Know My Mind," "Sunny Side of the Mountain," "Wild Side of Life," "I'm Thinking Tonight of My Blue Eyes," "Great Speckled Bird," the verse (but not the chorus) of "Footprints in the Snow," and "I Wonder Where You Are Tonight."

I–IV–I–V–I: Countless bluegrass songs share this progression, although the measure count varies widely. Some of the bigger hits include "Mountain Dew," "Amazing Grace," "Will the Circle Be Unbroken," "Bury Me Beneath the Willow," "Foggy Mountain Top," "Nine Pound Hammer," "White Dove," "My Rose of Old Kentucky," "White House Blues," "I'll Fly Away," and "The Wreck of Old 97."

Hank Williams' "I Saw the Light," below, is a typical example. The verse and chorus both go I–IV–I–V–I:

I SAW THE LIGHT—Key of E

TRACK 13

THE 12-BAR BLUES FORM

The blues was almost certainly brought to America by African slaves, and it quickly permeated nearly all musical genres as far back as the 1700s. It still does today, and bluegrass has always had its share of the blues. That means bluegrass melodies often have "blue notes"—i.e., ♭3rds, ♭5ths, and ♭7ths. It also means many songs forsake the typical 16- or 32-measure structure (or some multiple of eight) and adopt the 12-bar pattern popularized by countless blues musicians.

There are many variations of the 12-bar blues, but in its simplest form, it consists of three four-measure phrases. Often, the first two phrases have the same lyric, and the third phrase rhymes with the first two:

- First phrase: four measures of I

- Second phrase: two measures of IV, two measures of I

- Third phrase: two measures of V, two measures of I

Jimmie Rodgers, the 1930s super star who is often called "the father of country music," sang many 12-bar blues tunes, although he often added a few extra bars to create suspense. "'T' for Texas" was his earliest hit, and the following Rodgers tune, "California Blues," has also been recorded by many country and bluegrass artists. Like all of his blues tunes, it's numbered ("Blue Yodel #4 [California Blues]" is the title). Rodgers popularized yodeling; he was probably the first country artist to yodel. In "Blue Yodel #4 (California Blues)," there's a four-measure yodel at the end of each 12-bar verse.

Seventh chords have a bluesy sound and are often played in blues tunes instead of major chords. Here are the seventh chords you'll need for "California Blues":

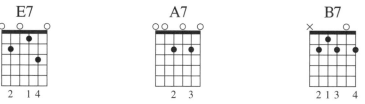

BLUE YODEL #4 (CALIFORNIA BLUES)—Key of E

TRACK 14

Words and Music by Jimmie Rodgers
Copyright © 1929 by Peer International Corporation
Copyright Renewed
International Copyright Secured   All Rights Reserved

USING THE CAPO

Although some songs, especially fiddle tunes, have "traditional keys," any song can be played in any key. The singer's vocal range is usually a determining factor in picking a key. So the bluegrass guitarist has to be prepared to play in any key, including guitar-unfriendly keys like B, F, or E♭. These keys require lots of barre chords, but the bluegrass guitar sound requires that ringing, sustaining tone you only get by playing open strings and first-position chords. That's why a bluegrass guitarist needs a capo: It allows him/her to "cheat" (capos used to be called "cheaters") and use easy, first-position chords in any key.

Many shapes and styles of capos can be found in music stores (see below), but they all do the same thing: Once you clamp the capo at, say, the 2nd fret, it's as if the guitar begins at that fret. Try it, and three things are immediately apparent:

- The first two frets are unusable.

- Every chord shape sounds two frets higher. Your G chord position now sounds an A chord, your C chord sounds like D, and so on.

- You can play a G run, and it's really an A run!

Shubb "Original" Capo   Kyser "Quick Change" Capo

Best of all, the capo helps you play in difficult keys. The chart below shows how to use the capo to play in any key using easy, first-position chords. It offers choices for most keys. For example, to play in the key of B♭, you can capo at the 1st fret, and the first-position A chord then becomes a B♭ chord. Or you can capo at the 3rd fret and play a first-position G chord, which then sounds like B♭.

CAPO CHART

To play in the key of	capo at fret #	and play a 1st position
A♭	1	G
	4	E
A	2	G
	5	E
B♭	1	A
	3	G
B	2	A
	4	G
C	3	A
	5	G
D♭	1	C
	4	A

To play in the key of	capo at fret #	and play a 1st position
D	2	C
E♭	1	D
	3	C
E	2	D
	4	C
F	1	E
	3	D
	5	C
G♭	2	E
	4	D
	6	C
G	3	E
	7	C

Once you have used the above capo chart to find your I chord, use the chord family chart, below, to find the IV and V chords:

CHORD FAMILY CHART

I chord	IV chord	V chord
A♭	D♭	E♭
A	D	E
B♭	E♭	F
B	E	F#
C	F	G
D♭	G♭	A♭
D	G	A
E♭	A♭	B♭
E	A	B
F	B♭	C
G♭	C♭ (B)	D♭
G	C	D

Suppose you want to play in the key of B, a popular bluegrass key. The capo chart says that if you capo at the 4th fret, the first-position G chord shape is your I chord (B). The chord family chart says that C and D are the IV and V chords that go with the G (I) chord. It also says that, since the capoed G chord is really a B, the IV and V chords are really E and F#.

Once you've practiced all the backup techniques (strums, bass runs, tag endings) in all keys, it's time to move on to soloing.

SOLOING

When it's time to play a solo, you have at least three choices:

1. Play the song's melody.
2. Play an altered or embellished melody.
3. Improvise freely, playing any melodies or licks that fit the song's chord progression.

The melody is a good place to begin. To play the melody, the first thing you need is familiarity with major scales.

FIRST-POSITION MAJOR SCALES

Because so many melodies are based on the major scale, if you know how to play it, you can pick out thousands of melodies by ear… without reading them! A *first-position major scale* is a scale that is played within the first four frets of the guitar. It includes open strings as well as fretted strings.

C MAJOR SCALE

Here's the first-position C major scale. Play it as written (up and down the scale) with a steady rhythm, over and over, until you can do it quickly and automatically.

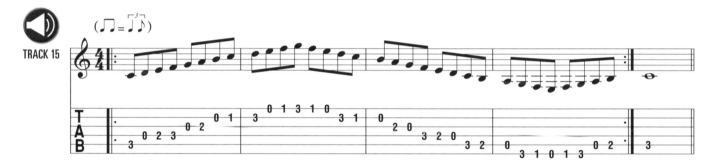

The bluegrass standard, "The Wreck of the Old 97," tells the story of a 1903 Virginia train wreck. The [A] section of the arrangement is the unadorned melody, which consists of C major scale notes. The [B] section includes Carter-style down/up strumming on the treble strings to fill out the rhythm.

THE WRECK OF THE OLD 97—Key of C

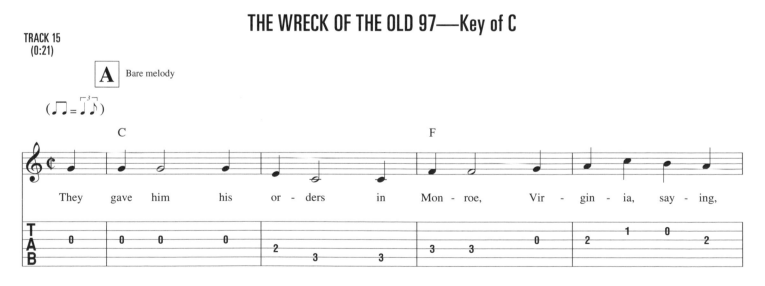

"Steve, you're way be - hind time._____ This is not thir - ty - eight, it's num - ber nine - ty - sev - en. You must put her in - to Spen - cer on time."

B Carter-Style arrangement

UPSTROKES AND DOWNSTROKES

Because all the melody notes in the previous arrangement are quarter or half notes, they are all played with downstrokes. The next arrangement has some more rapid melody notes, called *eighth notes* (in the third measure, for example). In order to play sequences of eighth notes with good rhythmic swing, alternate down- and upstrokes, picking down on the downbeats and up on the upbeats, like this:

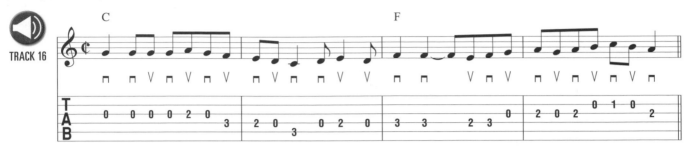

"My Rose of Old Kentucky" is a popular Bill Monroe tune. Once again, here's the bare melody of the verse, followed by a Carter-style arrangement. Both are in the key of C. (If a song has a chorus with a different melody than the verse, the verse is usually played as a solo, between vocals.)

MY ROSE OF OLD KENTUCKY—Key of C

TRACK 16
(0:13)

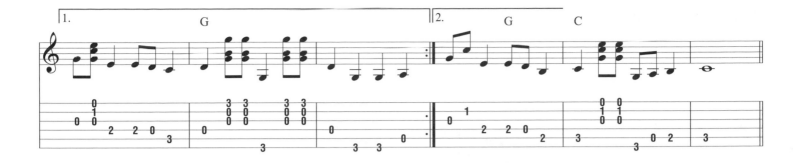

Fiddle tunes turn up in nearly every bluegrass set at concerts and jam sessions. They are also great major-scale picking exercises. "Arkansas Traveler" is one of the most popular of the older fiddle tunes (many of them go back 150 years or more). The "traditional key" is D, but here it is in C. You could play this arrangement with a fiddler if you put your capo on the 2nd fret.

Most fiddle tunes (including "Arkansas Traveler") have two sections, each played twice in a row. Sometimes they're called the "A section" and "B section," or "verse" and "chorus." Once you have played AABB, you've gone "once around the tune." In a band or a jam session, players take turns playing AABB.

TRACK 17

ARKANSAS TRAVELER—Key of C

G MAJOR SCALE

The first-position G major scale differs only from C major by one note (the F is sharped). Practice it as you did the C major scale, then play the key-of-G arrangement of "The Wreck of the Old 97" that follows.

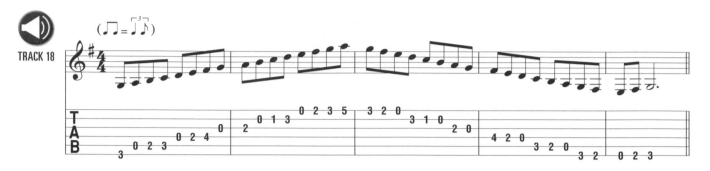

THE WRECK OF THE OLD 97—Key of G

TRACK 18
(0:14)

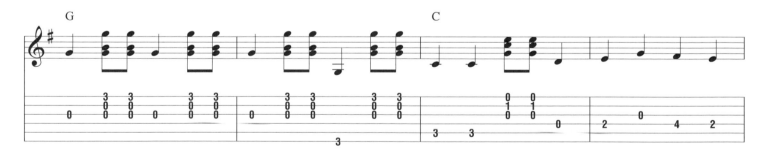

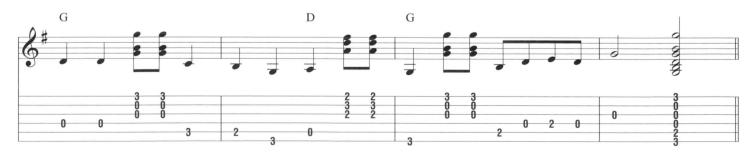

Here's "My Rose of Old Kentucky" in G:

MY ROSE OF OLD KENTUCKY—Key of G

TRACK 19

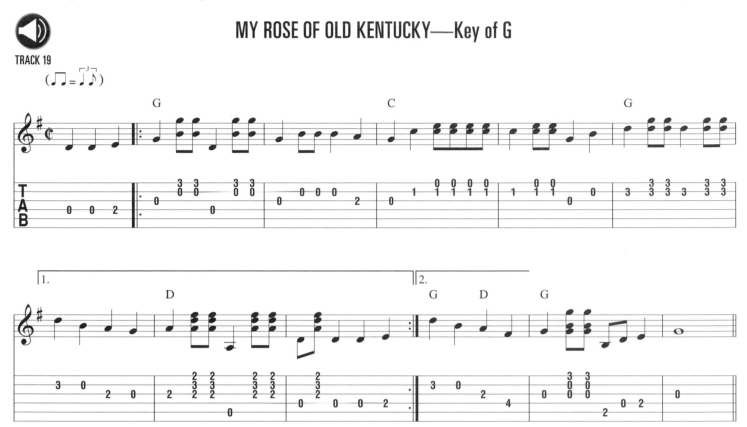

"Cripple Creek" is another centuries-old fiddle tune almost every bluegrass picker plays. Nearly every banjo player plays some version of it. The traditional key is A, so capo this arrangement at the 2nd fret when you encounter a purist:

CRIPPLE CREEK—Key of G

TRACK 20

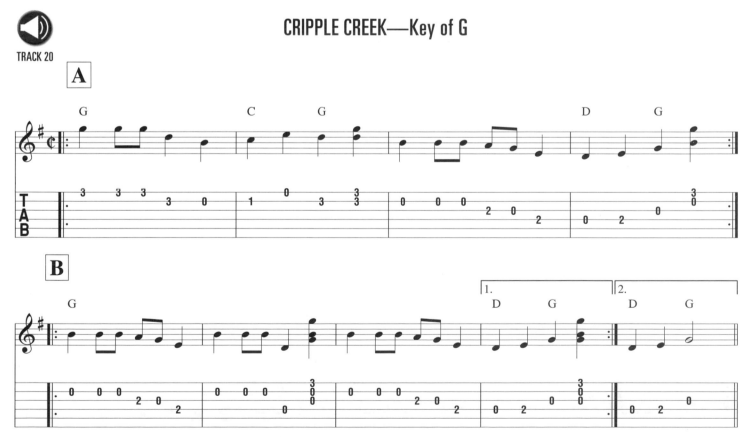

D MAJOR SCALE

The D major scale differs by only one note from the G major scale: it includes a C#. Practice the scale, then play our two standards, "The Wreck of the Old 97" and "My Rose of Old Kentucky."

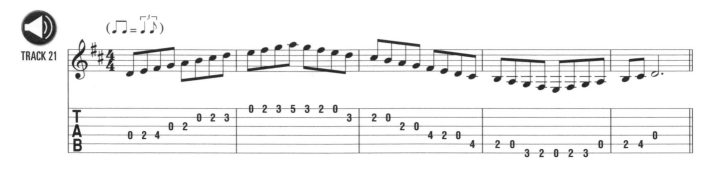

THE WRECK OF THE OLD 97—Key of D

TRACK 21
(0:16)

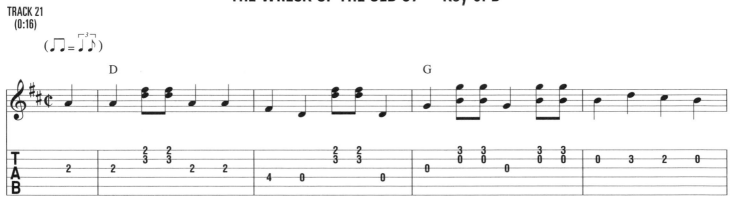

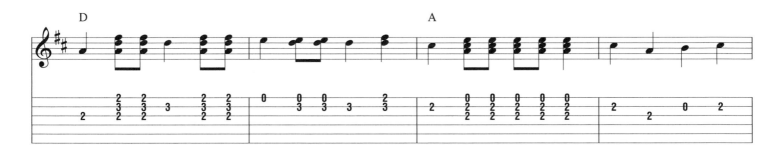

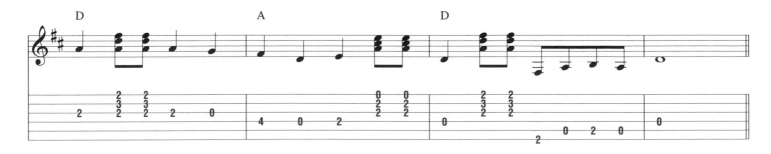

Here's "My Rose of Old Kentucky" in D:

MY ROSE OF OLD KENTUCKY—Key of D

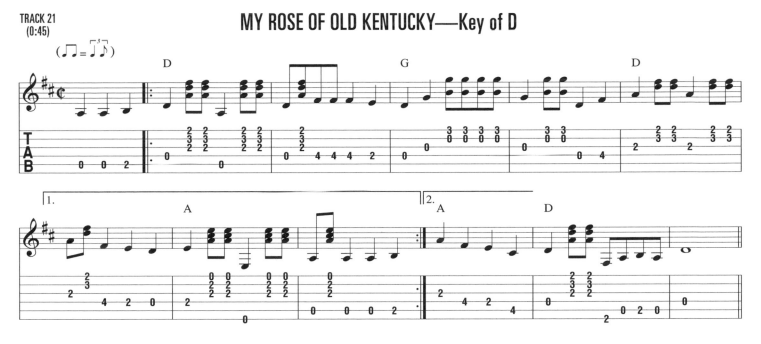

This version of "Arkansas Traveler" is in its traditional key of D:

ARKANSAS TRAVELER—Key of D

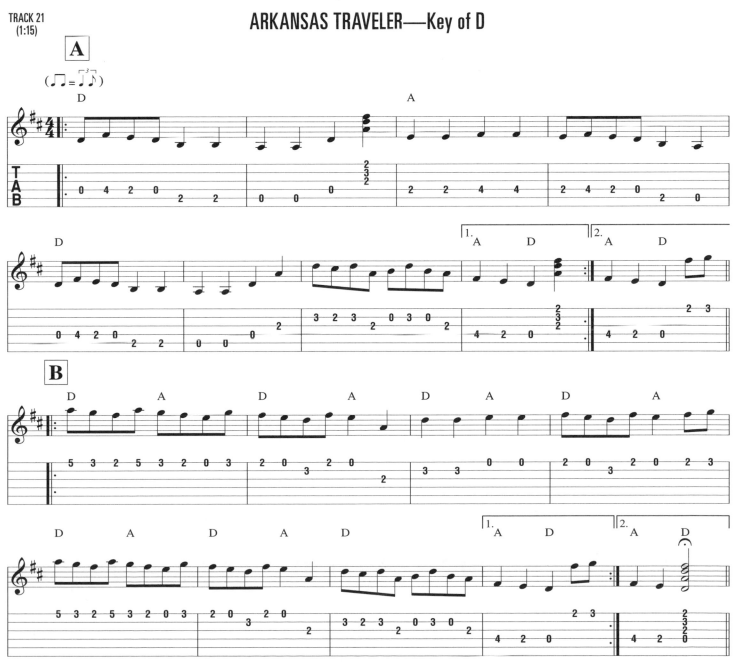

A MAJOR SCALE

The A major scale is just like D major, but with one more sharp: G♯. After you practice the scale, play the solos that follow. Just for a change, here are two new songs: "How Mountain Girls Can Love," made famous by the Stanley Brothers, and "Way Downtown," popularized by Doc Watson.

HOW MOUNTAIN GIRLS CAN LOVE—Key of A

The arrangement of "Way Downtown" includes an unusual fingering for the A chord. It makes certain melodies easier to play when strumming Carter-style in A:

WAY DOWNTOWN—Key of A

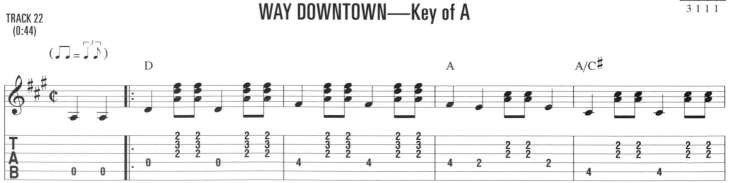

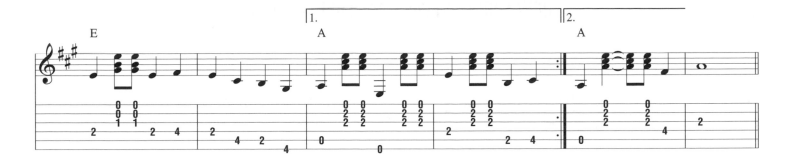

Here's an arrangement of "Cripple Creek" in A, its traditional key:

CRIPPLE CREEK—Key of A

TRACK 22
(1:12)

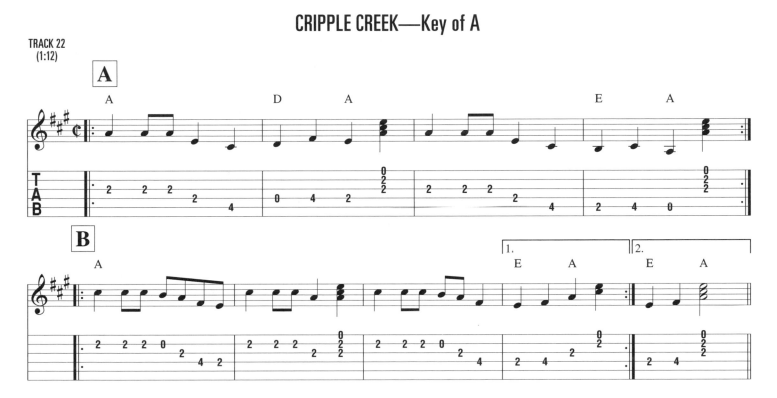

E MAJOR SCALE

The E major scale has the same notes as A major, except the D is sharp. Practice the E scale and the key-of-E arrangements of "How Mountain Girls Can Love" and "Way Downtown."

TRACK 23

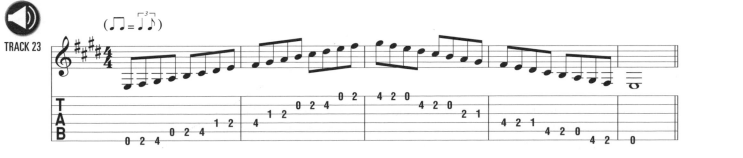

In the two arrangements that follow, and other tunes in the key of E, these two fingerings for B make melody notes more accessible than the first-position B7:

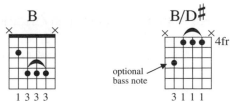

HOW MOUNTAIN GIRLS CAN LOVE—Key of E

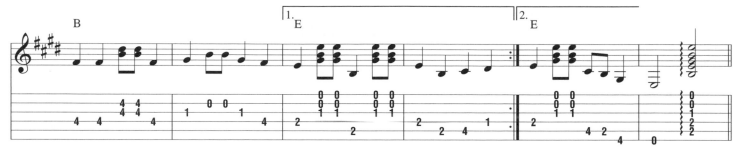

WAY DOWNTOWN—Key of E

HAMMER-ONS

There are very few frills or embellishments in the previous solos. The melody is played Carter-style, very literally. Most players alter and interpret a melody when they play a solo, and one embellishment technique they use is the *hammer-on*. With this technique, a note is sounded with the fretting hand instead of the picking hand.

For example, pick the open 4th string (D) and forcefully fret it (hammer-on) at the 2nd fret. If you do it properly, you hear two separate notes (D and E), even though you only picked one note. In tablature, hammer-ons are indicated with an arc, or *slur*—a curved line that connects one note (number) to another.

TRACK 24

In the following arrangement of "My Rose of Old Kentucky," most of the hammer-ons help the guitarist imitate the way the song is *sung*. They happen where syllables are stressed. The hammer-on at the end of the solo is part of a tag ending.

MY ROSE OF OLD KENTUCKY—Key of C

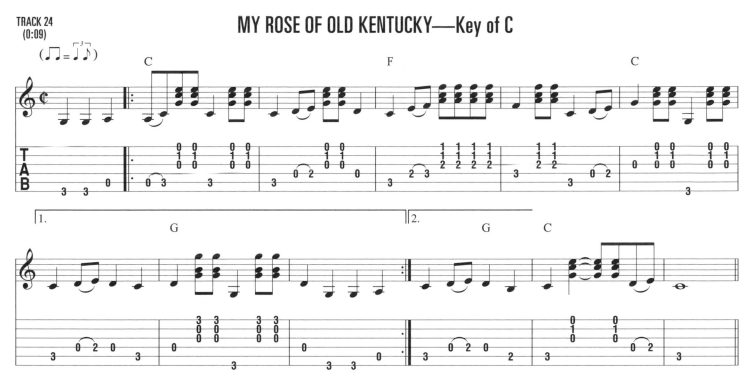

The following version of "Way Downtown" features a partial G chord and an A7 formation that both allow for effective hammer-ons:

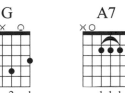

WAY DOWNTOWN—Key of D

You can also hammer on to a string that you haven't picked, as in the following sequence:

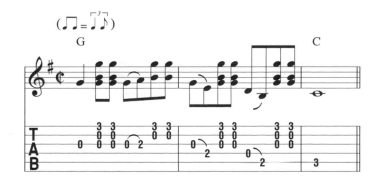

PULL-OFFS

Pull-offs are performed by plucking a note with your fretting hand. For example, fret the E string at the 3rd fret with your middle finger and at the 2nd fret with your index finger. Pick that string as usual, with your picking hand, then pluck down with the fretting index finger to sound the 2nd fret (F♯). Like hammer-ons, pull-offs are indicated in tablature with an arc connecting two notes (numbers). If the second number is higher, the arc indicates a hammer-on; if the second note is lower, there's a pull-off.

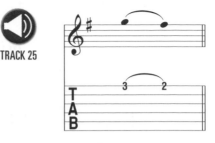

In the following version of "How Mountain Girls Can Love," hammer-ons and pull-offs imitate the way a singer stresses certain notes and add little embellishments to the song's melody.

HOW MOUNTAIN GIRLS CAN LOVE—Key of G

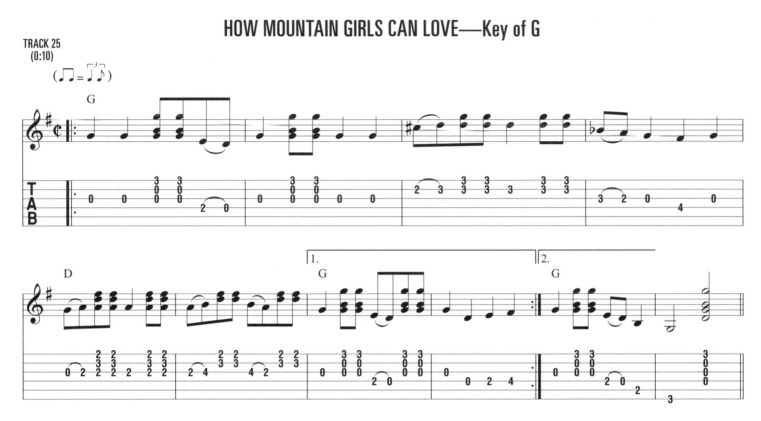

This solo uses hammer-ons and pull-offs to embellish the melody of "I Saw the Light."

I SAW THE LIGHT—Key of G

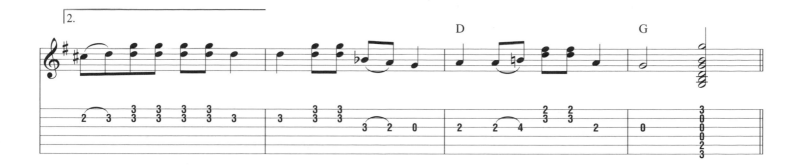

Pull-offs and hammer-ons add to this solo for "The Long Black Veil."

THE LONG BLACK VEIL—Key of C

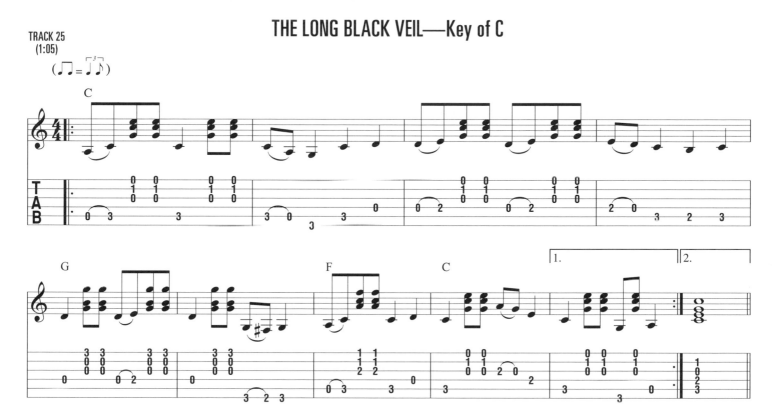

SLIDES

Slides are another way to embellish solos. You can slide up to a melody note from one or two frets back, or down to the note from one or two frets above it. Either way, it puts emphasis on the "destination note." You can also connect two melody notes with a slide. Here's how the various types of slides are indicated in tablature/music:

This version of "Cripple Creek" is enhanced with slides:

TRACK 26
(0:10)

CRIPPLE CREEK—Key of A

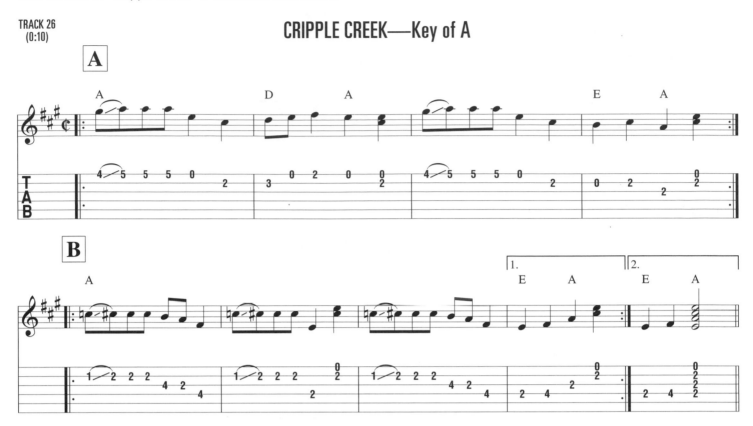

This "Salty Dog Blues" solo employs slides, hammer-ons, and pull-offs, but still sticks close to the melody:

TRACK 26
(0:40)

SALTY DOG BLUES—Key of G

Johnnie and Jack, who had a series of country hits during the 1950s, popularized "Ashes of Love," and it has become a bluegrass standard. The [A] section of this melodic solo presents the bare melody; the [B] section includes slides, hammer-ons, and pull-offs. Notice how you can stress an open-string note by sliding up to the same note on a lower string (as in measure 3 of the [B] section):

ASHES OF LOVE—Key of D

TRACK 27

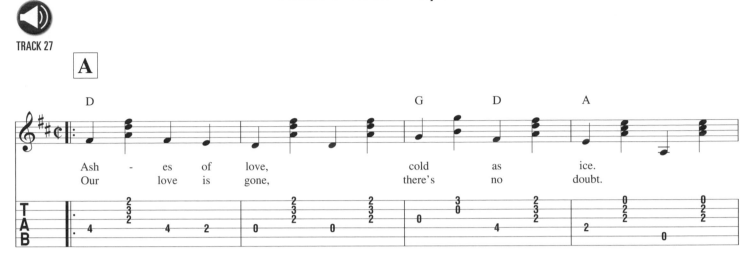

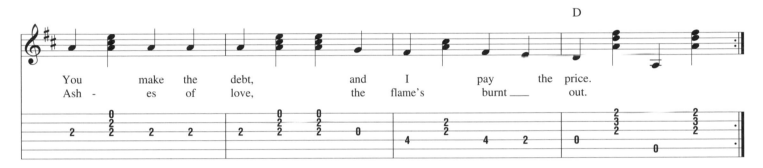

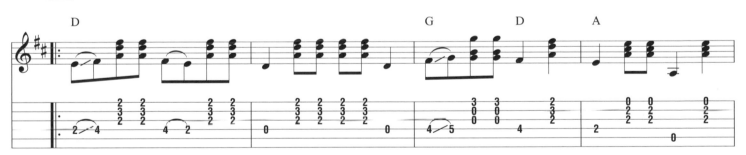

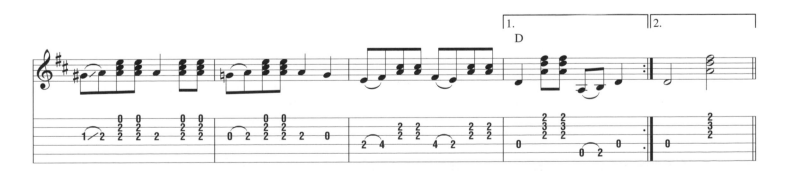

ADDING BLUE NOTES

As Bill Monroe often said, "There's a lot of blues in bluegrass." If the blues inflection isn't written into a song's melody, soloists and singers will often add "blue notes" (♭3rds, ♭5ths, and ♭7ths) to raise a song's blues quotient. Take another look at the first-position major scales and learn how to add blue notes to them.

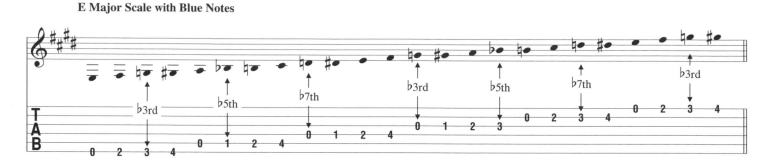

Once you know where the blue notes are, you can use them much as you did the slides, hammer-ons, and pull-offs to emphasize a melody note. You can play a blue note that's a fret below a major scale/melody note and slide or hammer on to the "real" note.

"You Don't Know My Mind" was made famous by Jimmy Martin, one of the great tenor singers and rhythm guitarists of bluegrass's "golden age." Here's the basic melody in the key of E:

TRACK 28

YOU DON'T KNOW MY MIND—Key of E

This next arrangement of "You Don't Know My Mind" features some bluesy embellishments:

YOU DON'T KNOW MY MIND—Key of E

TRACK 28
(0:40)

Here's the C major scale with blue notes, followed by a bluesy, key-of-C version of "You Don't Know My Mind."

C Major Scale with Blue Notes

YOU DON'T KNOW MY MIND—Key of C

TRACK 28
(1:17)

"I Am a Man of Constant Sorrow" lends itself to bluesy embellishments. Study the A major scale with blue notes, below. Then play the basic melodic version in A, followed by a bluesy version, including a "blues" tag ending.

A Major Scale with Blue Notes

TRACK 29

I AM A MAN OF CONSTANT SORROW—Key of A

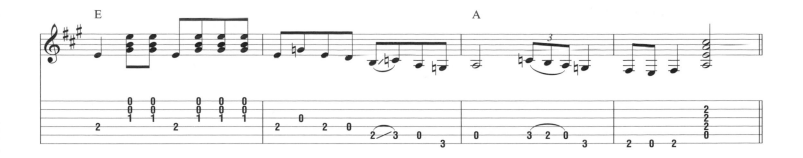

Here are two more bluesy solos of "I Am a Man of Constant Sorrow"—one in G and the other in D. Become familiar with the blue notes in each key before playing the arrangements.

G Major Scale with Blue Notes

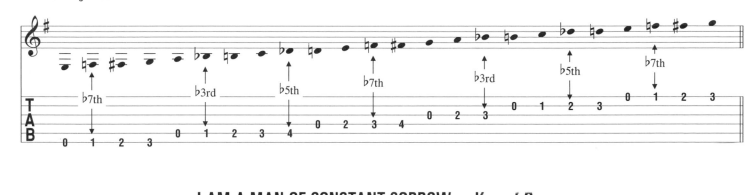

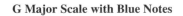

I AM A MAN OF CONSTANT SORROW—Key of G

TRACK 29
(0:51)

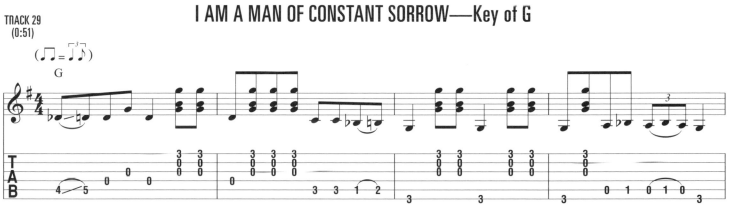

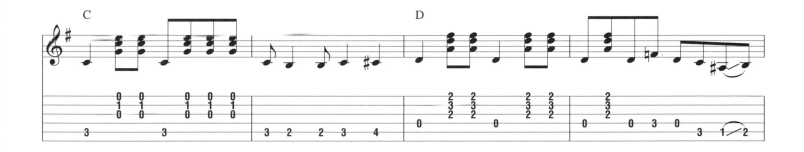

D Major Scale with Blue Notes

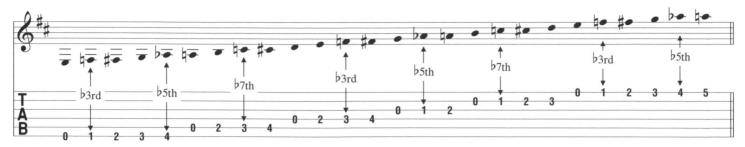

TRACK 29
(1:16)

I AM A MAN OF CONSTANT SORROW—Key of D

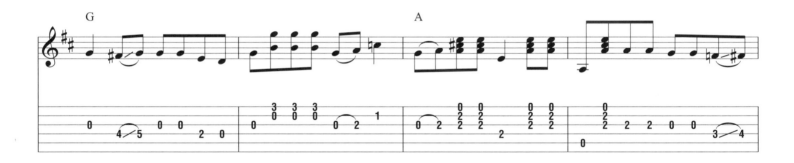

ORNAMENTING THE MELODY

Besides accenting melody notes with hammer-ons, pull-offs, slides, and adding blue notes, the soloist can ornament a melody by surrounding it with "extra" notes. These notes come from the song's major scale, although blue notes can be used as well. They are usually nearby neighbors of the given melody notes.

There are as many ways to ornament a melody as your imagination allows. Here are some common techniques:

- Lengthen a melodic phrase by starting it earlier with "lead-in" notes.

- Extend a melodic phrase; make it continue several notes longer than the basic melody.

- Play "between the melody notes" when there's room. If the melody involves quarter notes, add "in-between notes" to create eighth-note phrases.

- Play between the melodic phrases with *fills*.

Sometimes there's so much ornamentation that the melody gets buried or lost—there's no rule against that!

One very common ornamentation in bluegrass is the "kickoff" phrase that begins a solo. For example, the melody to "The Wreck of the Old 97," in the key of G, starts on a D note, but you can "lead up" to the D note like this:

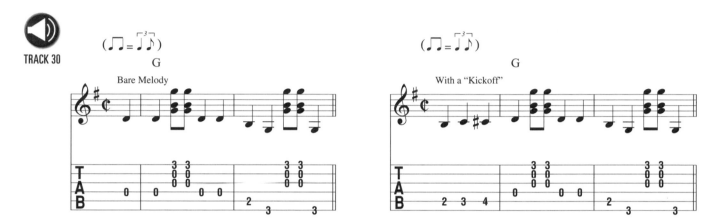

TRACK 30

The idea is to back up a few scale notes prior to the given note. The kickoffs in the solos that follow will give you a better idea of how to construct this type of "solo intro."

The arrangement of "The Wreck of the Old 97" includes all these ornamenting devices. There's a key-of-C version and a G version.

THE WRECK OF THE OLD 97—Keys of C and G

TRACK 31

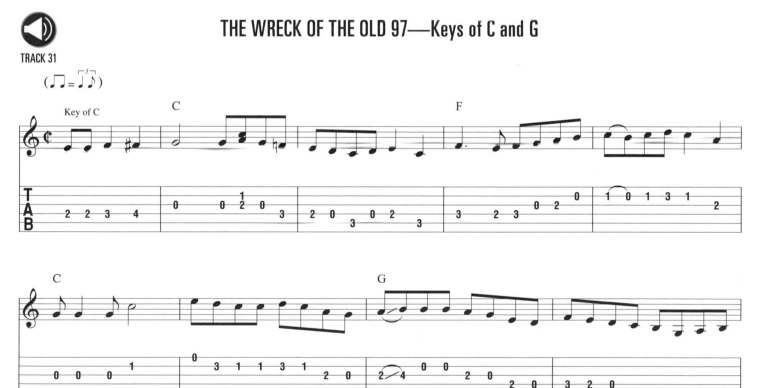

49

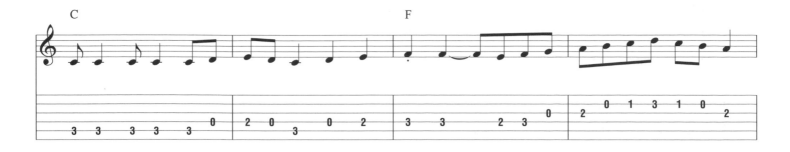

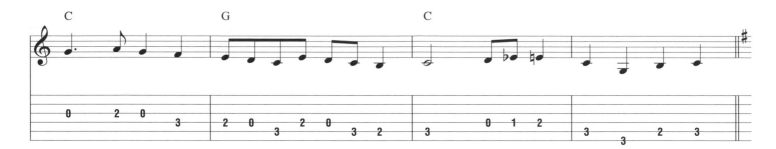

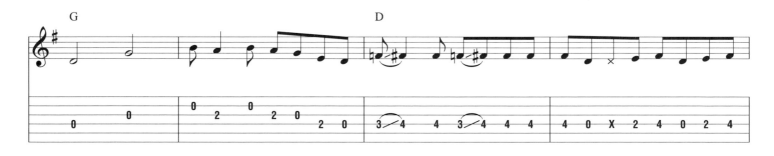

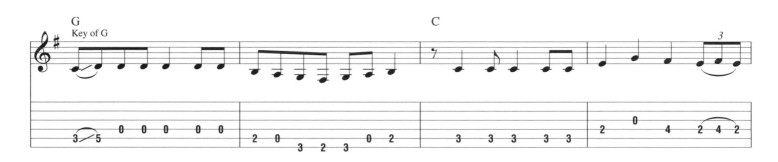

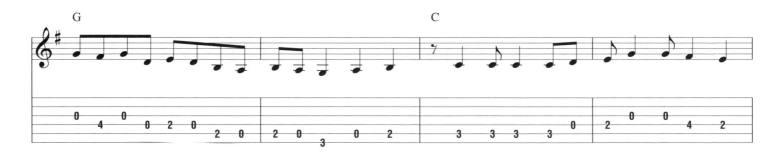

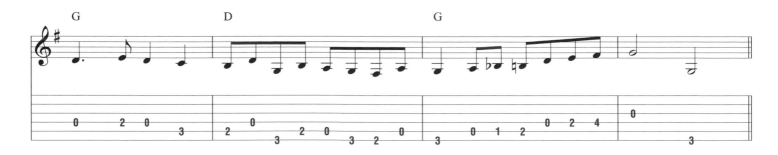

Here's "Ashes of Love" in D with melodic ornamentation:

ASHES OF LOVE—Key of D

TRACK 32

This key-of-A version of "My Rose of Old Kentucky" has a lot of ornamentaion:

MY ROSE OF OLD KENTUCKY—Key of A

TRACK 32
(0:34)

CROSSPICKING

Playing with the Stanley Brothers in the 1950s, George Shuffler popularized a flatpicking guitar technique that resembled the sound of bluegrass banjo rolls. It came to be known as *crosspicking*. Some call it "McReynolds style," referring to mandolinist Jesse McReynolds, who took the style to new heights a few years after Shuffler, playing with Jim & Jesse and the Virginia Boys. Clarence White, Doc Watson, and other guitarists utilized crosspicking in the early 1960s, and many pickers have adapted it to their own styles ever since.

With crosspicking, the melody is usually played on lower strings and embellished with rolls on the higher strings. Most pickers use eight-beat rolls divided into a 1–2–3–1–2–3–1–2 rhythm. There are many ways the roll can work. These three patterns are variations of the 5-string banjo's "forward rolls."

TRACK 33

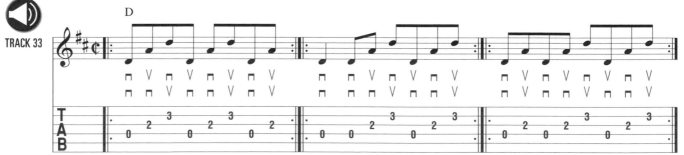

Since these rapid rolls are played with a flatpick, they require some fancy down- and upstroke patterns. Every player has his or her own method of dealing with this. The previous example gives two picking options. Try the strict down–up pattern first, then try the alternate pattern shown below it.

Here's a crosspicking version of "We'll Meet Again Sweetheart" in D, using forward roll crosspicking patterns:

TRACK 33
(0:27)

WE'LL MEET AGAIN SWEETHEART—Key of D

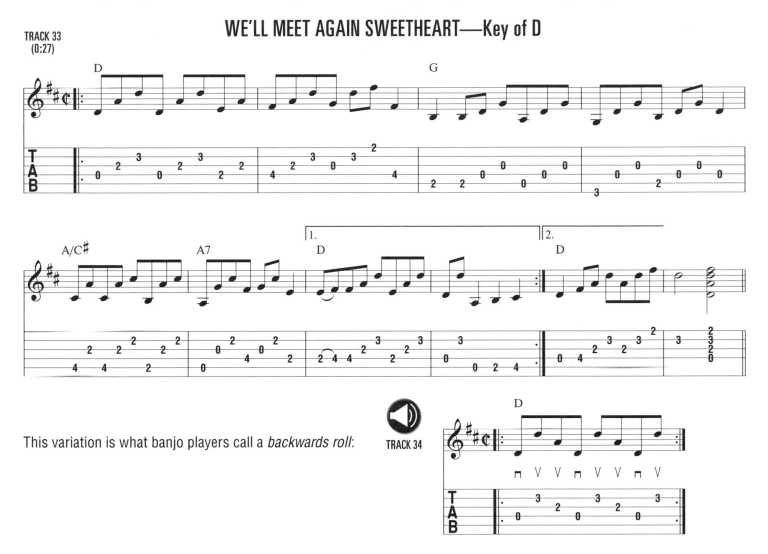

This variation is what banjo players call a *backwards roll*:

TRACK 34

The following version of "We'll Meet Again Sweetheart" makes use of backwards crosspicking patterns:

WE'LL MEET AGAIN SWEETHEART—Key of G

TRACK 34
(0.13)

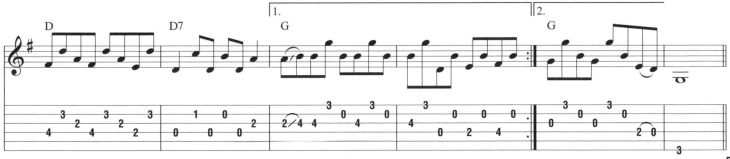

MOVEABLE MAJOR SCALES

The three moveable major scale patterns, below, enable you to play scale-based solos all over the fretboard in at least three different registers for any key. They are based on these three moveable chord positions:

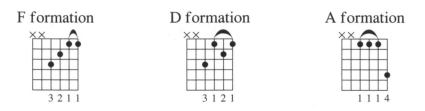

The G major scale, below, is based on the F formation:

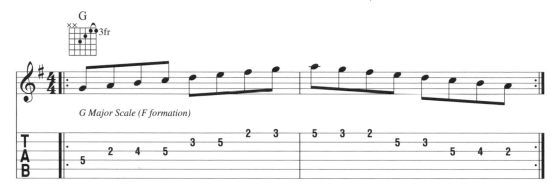

This higher-register G major scale is based on the D formation:

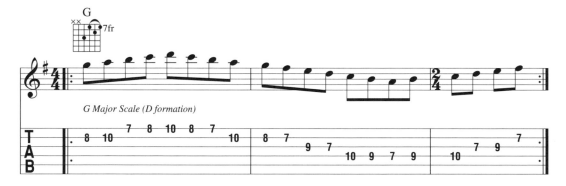

The still-higher-register G major scale is based on the A formation:

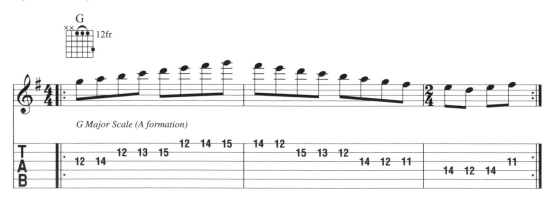

Locate the F formation by its root on the 1st or 4th strings. Once you learn the notes on either or both of these strings, you can play any chord using the F formation:

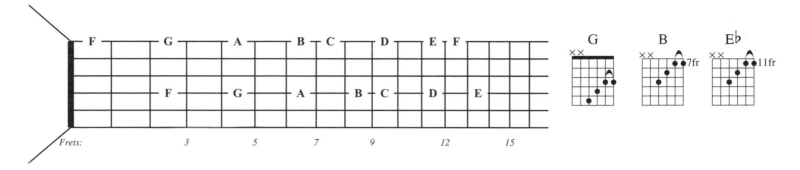

The root of the D formation is the 2nd string, so you can play D formations all over the fretboard if you memorize the notes on that string:

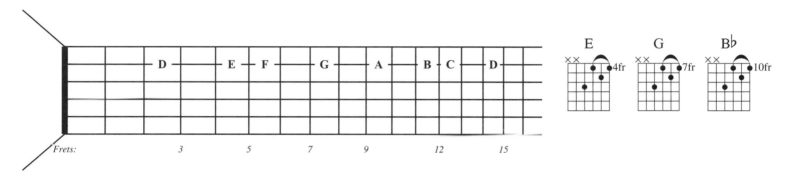

Locate the A formation by its 1st- or 3rd-string roots.

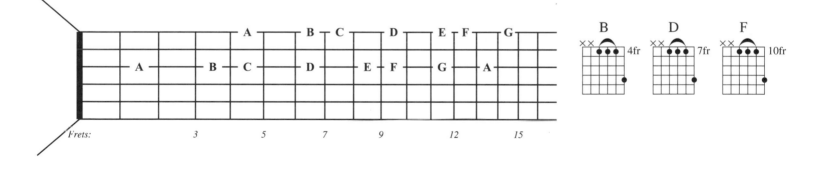

Use the F, D, and A formations to play any chord (G, D, E, etc.) three different ways. For example:

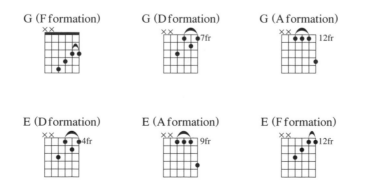

G (F formation)

G (D formation)

G (A formation)

E (D formation)

E (A formation)

E (F formation)

This solo to "The Long Black Veil" makes use of the D formation/G major scale. The A section presents the literal melody; the B section includes some ornamentation:

THE LONG BLACK VEIL—Key of G

TRACK 35

Here's "Arkansas Traveler" in D. The solo is based on the A formation:

ARKANSAS TRAVELER—Key of D

TRACK 36

In "The Wreck of the Old 97," the first half is the basic melody; the second half is embellished. The whole solo is in the key of A and uses the F formation.

THE WRECK OF THE OLD 97—Key of A

ADDING BLUE NOTES TO THE MOVEABLE MAJOR SCALES

These fretboard diagrams of the three moveable major chord formations include blue notes. The solos that follow include many bluesy ornaments.

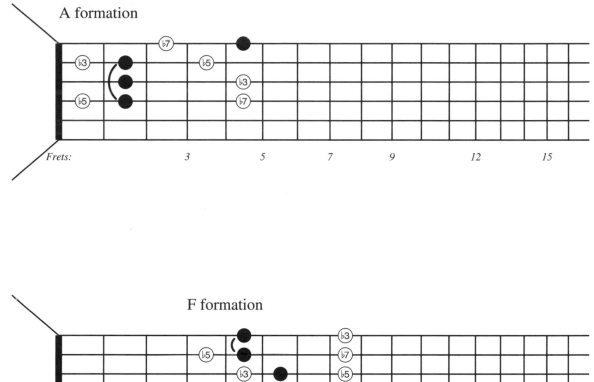

A formation

F formation

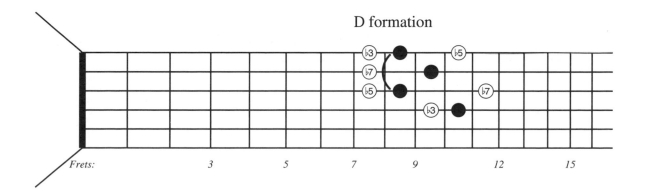

D formation

YOU DON'T KNOW MY MIND—Key of E

THE WRECK OF THE OLD 97—Key of A

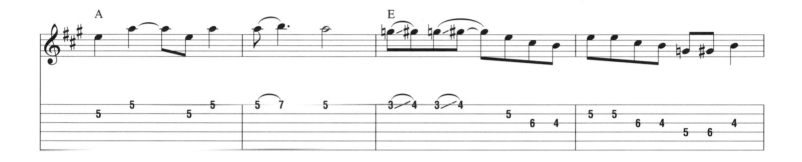

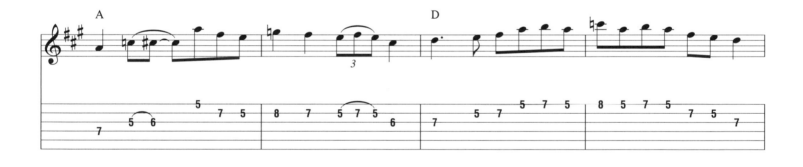

CHORD-BASED SOLOING UP THE NECK

Some solos are based on chords rather than scales. The soloist changes chord positions with the song's progression and makes up licks based on each chord change. The licks are based on each chord's major scale, and blue notes are also useful.

Here are the three major chord shapes, shown with "useful notes" surrounding them—both major scale notes and blue notes:

A formation

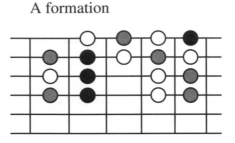

D formation

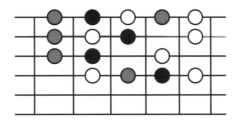

F formation

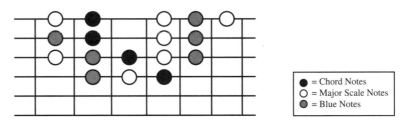

● = Chord Notes
○ = Major Scale Notes
● = Blue Notes

Here are two minor chord shapes and some "useful surrounding notes" that can be used to create licks and phrases:

Am formation

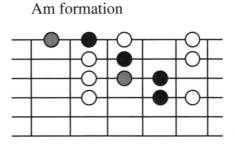

Fm formation

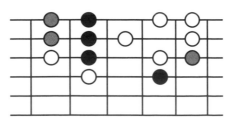

● = Chord Notes
○ = Major Scale Notes
● = Blue Notes

The following version of "Way Downtown" is chord-based, so there are occasional chord shapes mixed in with the single-note lines. The first half of the solo is an embellished melody, and the second half is improvised—the soloist invents an entirely new melody based on the song's chord progression.

WAY DOWNTOWN—Key of D

TRACK 39

"Salty Dog Blues," below, is a chord-based solo. Like the previous solo, the first half is ornamented melody; the second half is improvised.

SALTY DOG BLUES—Key of G

The following chord-based solo to "You Don't Know My Mind" barely makes reference to the song's melody at all. It's improvised and bluesy.

YOU DON'T KNOW MY MIND—Key of A

MAJOR PENTATONIC SCALES

The two moveable F major pentatonic scales diagrammed below provide another useful springboard for soloing. "Pentatonic" means "five tones," and these scales include five major-scale notes: root–2nd–3rd–5th–6th. They are moveable 6th-string and 5th-string root shapes. If you play them two frets higher (with a G root instead of F), you have two G major pentatonic scales.

Arrows are "slide" notes.

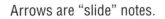
TRACK 42

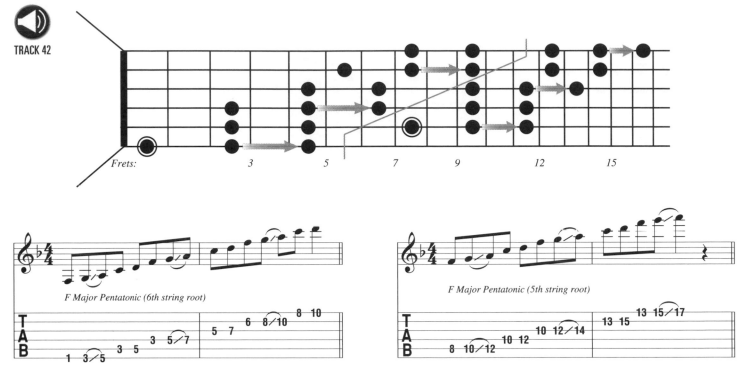

F Major Pentatonic (6th string root)

F Major Pentatonic (5th string root)

In both tunes that follow, the soloist changes scales "with the song's chord changes."

HOW MOUNTAIN GIRLS CAN LOVE—Key of F

TRACK 42
(0:22)

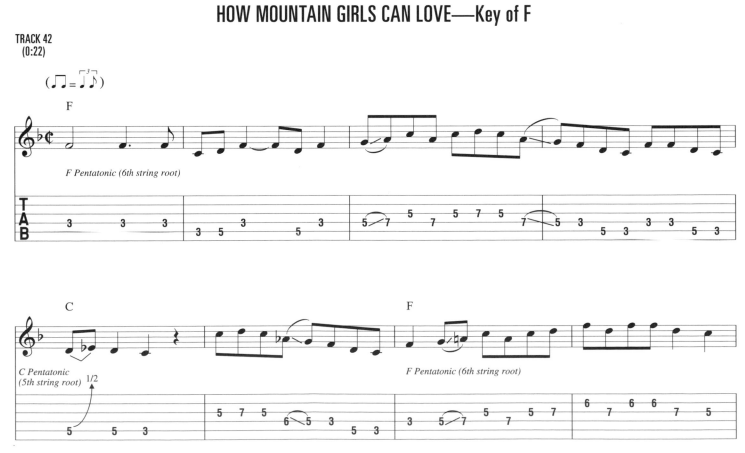

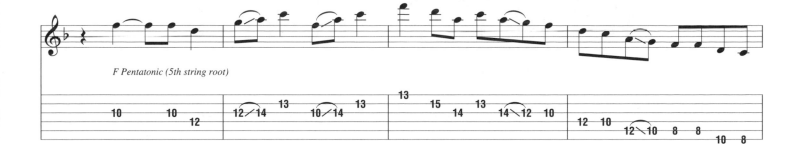

F Pentatonic (5th string root)

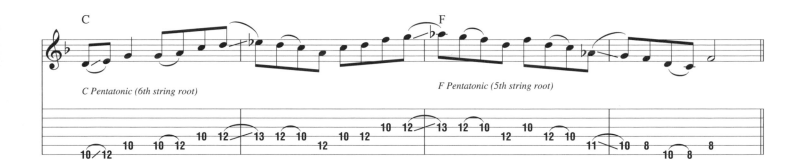

C

C Pentatonic (6th string root)

F

F Pentatonic (5th string root)

BLUE YODEL #4 (CALIFORNIA BLUES)—Key of C

TRACK 43

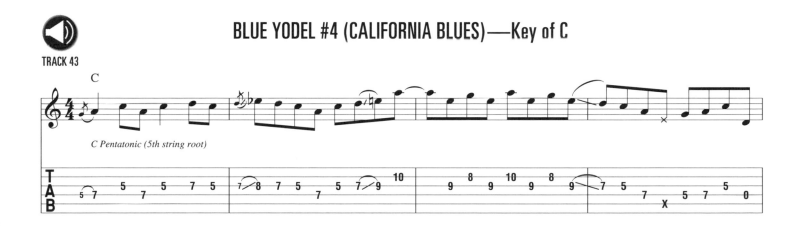

C

C Pentatonic (5th string root)

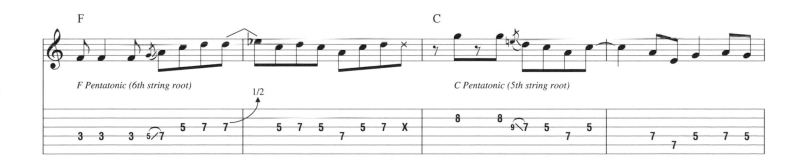

F

F Pentatonic (6th string root)

C

C Pentatonic (5th string root)

1/2

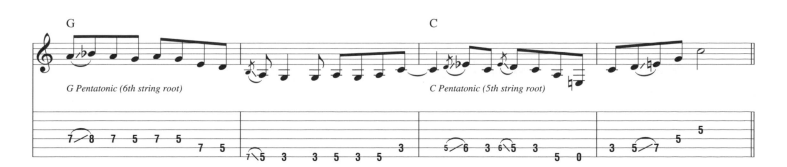

G

G Pentatonic (6th string root)

C

C Pentatonic (5th string root)

WHERE TO GO FROM HERE

To improve your backup and soloing skills, listen to contemporary and vintage bluegrass and play along with recordings. Here are some tips on playing along with recorded music:

1. Find the song's key. Listen for the I chord—it's the chord that gives you a feeling of resolution.

2. Listen to the bass! It usually plays the roots of chords, so it can help you find the I chord (the song's key) and the other chords as well.

3. When you've heard the I chord, play any formation on the guitar, such as the F formation at the 1st fret, and keep moving it around until it matches the I chord on the recording.

4. Once you've found the song's key, use your capo (if necessary) and capo chart so you can use first-position chords to play along.

5. Remember your I–IV–V chord families, and look for predictable chords and chord progressions.

Play along and try to match the groove you're hearing. If you're soloing, stick to one soloing strategy, such as first-position major scales, and give that concept a workout.

Playing with other people hones your chops as much as anything else while revealing your strengths and weaknesses—it shows you where you need improvement. It's also fun! Get together with friends who play bass, banjo, fiddle, mandolin, Dobro, or even guitar. Look online or call nearby music stores to find the nearest bluegrass jams. They're usually more cooperative than competitive, so don't be intimidated—get out there and play!

Good Luck,

Fred Sokolow

Fred Sokolow

Several of the author's Hal Leonard Publications are helpful for bluegrass guitarists, especially:

Fretboard Roadmaps for Bluegrass and Folk Guitar (book/CD)

The Carter Family Collection

The Jimmie Rodgers Collection

Gospel Guitar Songbook

Hank Williams Songbook

For more information on these and other Sokolow books, see *sokolowmusic.com*.

ABOUT THE AUTHOR

FRED SOKOLOW is a versatile "musician's musician." Besides fronting his own jazz, bluegrass, and rock bands, Fred has toured with Bobbie Gentry, Jim Stafford, Tom Paxton, Ian Whitcomb, Jody Stecher, and the Limeliters, playing guitar, banjo, mandolin, and Dobro. His music has been heard on many TV shows (*Survivor*, *Dr. Quinn*), commercials, and movies (listen for his Dixieland-style banjo in *The Cat's Meow*).

Sokolow has written over a hundred stringed-instrument books and videos for seven major publishers. This library of instructional material, which teaches jazz, rock, bluegrass, country, and blues guitar, banjo, ukulele, Dobro, and mandolin, is sold on six continents. He also teaches musical seminars on the West Coast. Two jazz CDs, two rock guitar, and two banjo recordings, which showcase Sokolow's technique, all received excellent reviews in the U.S. and Europe.

If you think Sokolow still isn't versatile enough, know that he emceed for Carol Doda at San Francisco's legendary Condor Club, accompanied a Russian balalaika virtuoso at the swank Bonaventure Hotel in L.A., won the "Gong Show," played lap steel and banjo on the "Tonight Show," picked Dobro with Chubby Checker, and played mandolin with Rick James.

Direct questions you may have about this book or other Fred Sokolow books to *sokolowmusic.com*.

GUITAR NOTATION LEGEND

Guitar music can be notated three different ways: on a *musical staff*, in *tablature*, and in *rhythm slashes*.

RHYTHM SLASHES are written above the staff. Strum chords in the rhythm indicated. Use the chord diagrams found at the top of the first page of the transcription for the appropriate chord voicings. Round noteheads indicate single notes.

THE MUSICAL STAFF shows pitches and rhythms and is divided by bar lines into measures. Pitches are named after the first seven letters of the alphabet.

TABLATURE graphically represents the guitar fingerboard. Each horizontal line represents a string, and each number represents a fret.

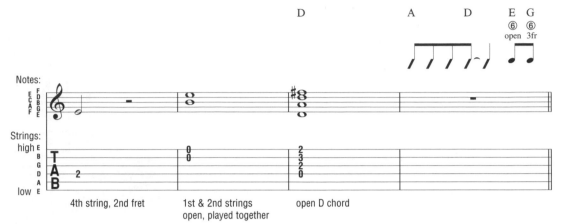

4th string, 2nd fret   1st & 2nd strings open, played together   open D chord

Definitions for Special Guitar Notation

HALF-STEP BEND: Strike the note and bend up 1/2 step.

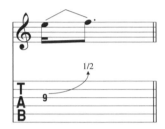

WHOLE-STEP BEND: Strike the note and bend up one step.

GRACE NOTE BEND: Strike the note and immediately bend up as indicated.

SLIGHT (MICROTONE) BEND: Strike the note and bend up 1/4 step.

BEND AND RELEASE: Strike the note and bend up as indicated, then release back to the original note. Only the first note is struck.

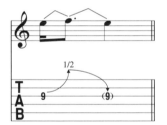

PRE-BEND: Bend the note as indicated, then strike it.

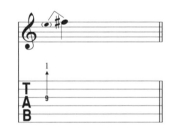

PRE-BEND AND RELEASE: Bend the note as indicated. Strike it and release the bend back to the original note.

UNISON BEND: Strike the two notes simultaneously and bend the lower note up to the pitch of the higher.

VIBRATO: The string is vibrated by rapidly bending and releasing the note with the fretting hand.

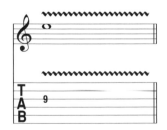

WIDE VIBRATO: The pitch is varied to a greater degree by vibrating with the fretting hand.

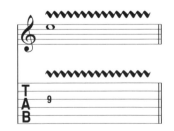

HAMMER-ON: Strike the first (lower) note with one finger, then sound the higher note (on the same string) with another finger by fretting it without picking.

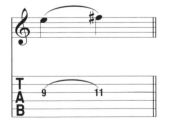

PULL-OFF: Place both fingers on the notes to be sounded. Strike the first note and without picking, pull the finger off to sound the second (lower) note.

LEGATO SLIDE: Strike the first note and then slide the same fret-hand finger up or down to the second note. The second note is not struck.

SHIFT SLIDE: Same as legato slide, except the second note is struck.

TRILL: Very rapidly alternate between the notes indicated by continuously hammering on and pulling off.

TAPPING: Hammer ("tap") the fret indicated with the pick-hand index or middle finger and pull off to the note fretted by the fret hand.

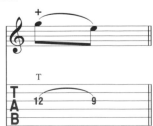

NATURAL HARMONIC: Strike the note while the fret-hand lightly touches the string directly over the fret indicated.

PINCH HARMONIC: The note is fretted normally and a harmonic is produced by adding the edge of the thumb or the tip of the index finger of the pick hand to the normal pick attack.

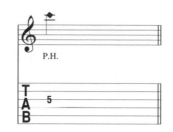

HARP HARMONIC: The note is fretted normally and a harmonic is produced by gently resting the pick hand's index finger directly above the indicated fret (in parentheses) while the pick hand's thumb or pick assists by plucking the appropriate string.

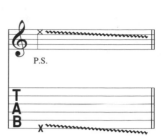

PICK SCRAPE: The edge of the pick is rubbed down (or up) the string, producing a scratchy sound.

MUFFLED STRINGS: A percussive sound is produced by laying the fret hand across the string(s) without depressing, and striking them with the pick hand.

PALM MUTING: The note is partially muted by the pick hand lightly touching the string(s) just before the bridge.

RAKE: Drag the pick across the strings indicated with a single motion.

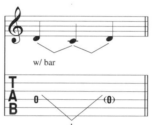

TREMOLO PICKING: The note is picked as rapidly and continuously as possible.

ARPEGGIATE: Play the notes of the chord indicated by quickly rolling them from bottom to top.

VIBRATO BAR DIVE AND RETURN: The pitch of the note or chord is dropped a specified number of steps (in rhythm), then returned to the original pitch.

VIBRATO BAR SCOOP: Depress the bar just before striking the note, then quickly release the bar.

VIBRATO BAR DIP: Strike the note and then immediately drop a specified number of steps, then release back to the original pitch.

Definitions for Special Guitar Notation

(accent)	• Accentuate note (play it louder).	
(accent)	• Accentuate note with great intensity.	
(staccato)	• Play the note short.	
⊓	• Downstroke	
V	• Upstroke	

D.S. al Coda • Go back to the sign (𝄋), then play until the measure marked "**To Coda**," then skip to the section labelled "**Coda**."

D.C. al Fine • Go back to the beginning of the song and play until the measure marked "***Fine***" (end).

Rhy. Fig. • Label used to recall a recurring accompaniment pattern (usually chordal).

Riff • Label used to recall composed, melodic lines (usually single notes) which recur.

Fill • Label used to identify a brief melodic figure which is to be inserted into the arrangement.

Rhy. Fill • A chordal version of a Fill.

tacet • Instrument is silent (drops out).

• Repeat measures between signs.

• When a repeated section has different endings, play the first ending only the first time and the second ending only the second time.

NOTE: Tablature numbers in parentheses mean:
1. The note is being sustained over a system (note in standard notation is tied), or
2. The note is sustained, but a new articulation (such as a hammer-on, pull-off, slide or vibrato) begins, or
3. The note is a barely audible "ghost" note (note in standard notation is also in parentheses).

Presenting the Best in
BLUEGRASS

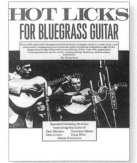

THE REAL BLUEGRASS BOOK

Ballad of Jed Clampett • Bill Cheatham • Down to the River to Pray • Foggy Mountain Top • I'm Goin' Back to Old Kentucky • John Henry • Old Train • Pretty Polly • Rocky Top • Sally Goodin • Wildwood Flower • and more.
00310910 C Instruments..............................$39.99

BLUEGRASS

Guitar Play-Along
Book/CD Pack
8 songs: Duelin' Banjos • Foggy Mountain Breakdown • Gold Rush • I Am a Man of Constant Sorrow • Nine Pound Hammer • Orange Blossom Special • Rocky Top • Wildwood Flower.
00699910 Guitar...$17.99

BLUEGRASS GUITAR

by Happy Traum
Book/CD Pack
This guitar workbook covers every aspect of bluegrass playing, from simple accompaniment to advanced instrumentals.
14004656 Guitar...$27.99

BLUEGRASS GUITAR CLASSICS

22 Carter-style solos: Back Up and Push • The Big Rock Candy Mountain • Cotton Eyed Joe • Cumberland Gap • Down Yonder • Jesse James • John Henry • Little Sadie Long Journey Home • Man of Constant Sorrow • Midnight Special • Mule Skinner Blues • Red Wing • Uncle Joe • The Wabash Cannon Ball • Wildwood Flower • and more.
00699529 Solo Guitar...................................$8.99

BLUEGRASS GUITAR

Arranged and Performed by Wayne Henderson
Transcribed by David Ziegele
Book/CD Pack
10 classic bluegrass tunes: Black Mountain Rag • Fisher's Hornpipe • Leather Britches • Lime Rock • Sally Anne • Take Me Out to the Ball Game • Temperence Reel • Twinkle Little Star • and more.
00700184 Guitar Solo..................................$16.99

BLUEGRASS SONGS FOR EASY GUITAR

25 bluegrass standards: Alabama Jubilee • Arkansas Traveler • Bill Cheatham • Blackberry Blossom • The Fox • Great Speckled Bird • I Am a Pilgrim • New River Train • Red Rocking Chair • Red Wing • Sally Goodin • Soldier's Joy • Turkey in the Straw • and more.
00702394 Easy Guitar with Notes & Tab.......$15.99

BLUEGRASS STANDARDS

by David Hamburger
16 bluegrass classics expertly arranged: Ballad of Jed Clampett • Blue Yodel No. 4 (California Blues) • Can't You Hear Me Calling • I'll Go Stepping Too • I'm Goin' Back to Old Kentucky • Let Me Love You One More Time • My Rose of Old Kentucky • We'll Meet Again Sweetheart • and more.
00699760 Solo Guitar...................................$7.99

FIRST 50 BLUEGRASS SOLOS YOU SHOULD PLAY ON GUITAR

arr. Fred Sokolow
Songs include: Arkansas Traveler • Cripple Creek • I Am a Man of Constant Sorrow • I'll Fly Away • Long Journey Home • Molly and Tenbrooks • Old Joe Clark • The Red Haired Boy • Rocky Top • Wabash Cannonball • Wayfaring Stranger • You Don't Know My Mind • and more!
00298574 Solo Guitar.................................$15.99

FRETBOARD ROADMAPS – BLUEGRASS AND FOLK GUITAR

by Fred Sokolow
Book/CD Pack
This book/CD pack will have you playing lead and rhythm anywhere on the fretboard, in any key. You'll learn chord-based licks, moveable major and blues scales, major pentatonic "sliding scales," first-position major scales, and moveable-position major scales.
00695355 Guitar...$14.99

THE GUITAR PICKER'S FAKEBOOK

by David Brody
Compiled, edited and arranged by David Brody, this is the ultimate sourcebook for the traditional guitar player. It contains over 280 jigs, reels, rags, hornpipes and breakdowns from all the major traditional instrumental styles.
14013518 Melody/Lyrics/Chords.................$32.99

O BROTHER, WHERE ART THOU?

Songs include: Big Rock Candy Mountain (Harry McClintock) • You Are My Sunshine (Norman Blake) • Hard Time Killing Floor Blues (Chris Thomas King) • I Am a Man of Constant Sorrow (The Soggy Bottom Boys/Norman Blake) • Keep on the Sunny Side (The Whites) • I'll Fly Away (Alison Krauss and Gillian Welch) • and more.
00313182 Guitar...$22.99

HOT LICKS FOR BLUEGRASS GUITAR

by Orrin Star
Over 350 authentic bluegrass licks are included in this book, which also discusses how to apply the licks to create your own solos and expand your musical understanding and knowledge of the fingerboard.
14015430 Guitar Licks................................$26.99

HAL•LEONARD®
www.halleonard.com

Prices, contents, and availability subject to change.